—THE—
PROPERTY
DEVELOPERS
BLUEPRINT

How to Make Life Changing Money From
Just One Development Even If You Don't Have
Any Experience or Money

ANDY HUBBARD

Disclaimer

Author: Andy Hubbard

ISBN: 978-1-7384171-9-3

Category: Business / Property / Finance

"If you don't change what you are doing today, all of your tomorrows will look like yesterday." **- Jim Rohn.**

DEDICATION

I dedicate this book to my late father-in-law, Leonard Rawlings, a true hero whom I had the privilege of knowing and was fortunate to name a street after. Without this amazing man, I wouldn't have met my lovely wife, Sam, and our exceptionally talented boys, Luke and Lewis. They make up an amazing family that supports me in everything I do, even the crazy things you're about to find out.

FOREWORD

Dive into the realm of property development with Andy Hubbard's straightforward guide, a no-nonsense blueprint to forging your own fortune, brick by brick. Andy, a close friend of mine, is renowned as the UK's best in the business when it comes to teaching and mentoring, laying out the roadmap to your success.

From modest origins to a prominent figure in property development, he has traversed the path and amassed financial freedom – not only for himself but for future generations through the legacy he creates, helping ordinary people get extraordinary results.

With over three decades of experience and industry insight, Andy has been there and done it. He's trodden the path you are about to go down, meaning you can avoid the mistakes others make and fast-track your journey, ensuring you do things the right way.

While the prospect of property development may seem daunting, akin to scaling a mountain or venturing into uncharted waters, Andy is adept at conquering challenges. This book serves as your guiding compass, brimming with Andy's wisdom to transform your aspirations into your achievements.

Within this amazing book, you'll discover a wealth of advice intertwined with Andy's passion and dedication. His enthusiasm is beyond contagious, propelling you on a transformative journey way beyond what you could imagine and in quick time.

Whether you're a novice or seasoned veteran, this book is your gateway to the step-by-step system of property development. Brace yourself for a journey that will redefine not only you as a person but also your future that you've always been dreaming of.

Credit goes to Andy for assembling this invaluable resource and sharing what has made him a huge success, and to you for daring to turn dreams into reality.

Here's to constructing more than just buildings, here's to constructing a life beyond your wildest dreams with the life-changing property developers' blueprint.

Richard Stone

ACKNOWLEDGEMENTS

I'd like to thank my wife Sam, who, without her pushing me to attend a retreat back in 2015 in the Cayman Islands, you wouldn't be reading this book. She has always supported and believed in me when I wanted to do anything, and when I said I wanted to become a property developer, she was right behind me as always, no questions asked. She believes in everything I do and never doubts my abilities to succeed, and therefore I have a duty as a husband and best friend not to let her down.

I'd also like to thank my sons Luke and Lewis for turning out to be incredibly talented in many different areas, far greater than people twice their age. Those lads, who are like my best mates, can turn their hand to absolutely anything, and within hours, you would think they had been doing it for years. I'd like to think I've played a big part in passing my skills on and mindset down to my sons, but you can lead a horse to water as they say, so it's only right they take the credit for their skill set themselves that will serve them extremely well throughout life that I'm proud to be part of.

My parents also deserve huge credit for a very good upbringing whilst not having much money, teaching me what was right and wrong, good from bad, all the old-fashioned traits that the current world seems to have forgotten. Watching my Dad make and fix anything in his shed led me to a life of being creative and skilled with my hands for which I will be forever grateful. He had an attitude of "I can do it," which I have also embraced even though leveraging other people has now become the norm in business.

I must give a huge thank you to my mentors; these guys changed absolutely everything for me and my family. They guided me from working myself into an early grave and never seeing my family to having a life of freedom and an abundance of money. A life many could only dream of but has now come true. My mentors have shown me just how powerful it is to help others fulfil their dreams and ambitions through training and mentoring, ensuring my legacy lives on way beyond me. I wish I could say I met them sooner, but I did, 9 years before, but I never took action, something I regret looking back on, so never let this be you.

Some of us need that push, so be free to be pushed by your loved ones, even if this means getting out of your comfort zone. You never know where you may end up.

Table of Contents

INTRODUCTION

"It's not getting the million pounds that's important, it's what it makes of you to achieve becoming a millionaire" - **Jim Rohn.**

Ask yourself this question, would you like more time, freedom and money? Well, you're in the right place because I've written this book especially for you.

My wife Sam and many others have been telling me to write this book for a long time, so I thought for once I'd do what I was told and get on with it. I'll be sharing with you my rollercoaster journey where I went from being a busy tradesman working 80-100+ hour work weeks, never seeing my family, and on a road to destroying myself physically, to creating a lifestyle of pretty much doing what I want, when I want, with whom I want, and as much as I want. By sharing what I've learned here in this book, you and others can benefit in so many ways.

I want this book to allow you to understand that you don't have to go through life living pay check to pay check, never seeing your kids or your partner due to working long hours, not spending any time on your hobbies, and ruining your bodies doing repetitive physical work day in and day out. A life you've always dreamed of is definitely possible and not as far away as you may think with some small proven changes over a period of time. If someone like me, a bricklayer from Peterborough who failed miserably at school and had to start from zero, can do it, then certainly you can too.

One thing I've learned over the years is that once success has been achieved, it can be replicated, and if this is broken down into a simple step-by-step system, then anyone can copy and follow that system and achieve similar results, but in a much quicker time period. Following a system that works will fast track your results because you can avoid the mistakes others have made and go straight to the things that work and get the results you desire.

One of the key things I did back in 2015 was invest heavily in my own education, personal development, and mindset with mentors who have played a huge part in me being where I am today. I will be sharing their tips and secrets throughout this book. Spending six figures of your family's holiday money on yourself isn't for everyone, but I've since had a return on that investment many times over and will continue to do so forever. Investing in yourself is the very best investment you can make, and the sooner you do it, the sooner you will reap the rewards. This book is not just a book; it is an investment in your education. You will learn lots of new information here that is proven to work, start to look at things differently, and get results from implementing the steps one at a time.

The Property Development strategy has been a big part of my success, and just one deal can be truly life-changing for you. This is what I want you to keep at the forefront of your mind: just one deal. After repeating this on a number of deals, many people kept asking me to teach and show them how to do what I was doing. For this, I needed a system, and this is where the Property Developers Blueprint was born. Throughout this book, I will be sharing this proven eight-step system, plenty of tips and advice, plus some important exercises for you to do. Do not skip these as they will be key to changing your mindset and thinking bigger, certainly beyond your current limiting belief system.

So, who exactly is this book for?

It is for existing property investors, new or experienced, who have had enough of making small cash flow returns each month from their Buy to Lets, HMOs, serviced accommodations, Rent to Rents, etc. Can't get all of your money back out of every deal, don't enjoy managing tenants, don't want to wait 20-30 years for property to go up in value, and don't want to create a full-time job for themselves by being a landlord. Don't want to keep chasing rents, dealing with tenant issues, have their phone constantly ringing with problems, and want to do one deal at the top of the food chain rather than many smaller ones at the bottom. It's for any tradesmen who are busy working crazy hours like I used to, working for other developers (making them the profits while you get the wage) and those lovely customers who message and call you late evenings and weekends while you're sitting there with your loved ones (creating their dream home), trading your time for money, your body wearing out from backache, knee, shoulder, and elbow pains, want to leverage other people to do the work, want their weekends back, and more importantly want to spend time with their family or time on their hobbies.

This book is for anyone who feels stuck on the hamster wheel of life, hates their job/career, wants to earn more money, wants more time, wants more freedom, wants more for their family, wants to retire, wants a lifestyle, wants to pick and choose when they work, wants to build a new exciting proven business, wants the dream cars and holidays, wants to build their own dream home, and live life on their terms. Maybe you're at a crossroads and not sure which way to go, this book might just make that decision a lot easier for you going forward.

So why am I writing this long overdue book? My mentor told me "Andy, don't ever take your knowledge and experience to the grave without sharing it with as many people as possible on the planet. There are 2 main reasons, number 1, others can get to live an amazing life of freedom and choice like you do by following in your footsteps, and number 2, this book is part of your great legacy, it will keep on helping people long after you've gone."

I believe everyone can achieve financial freedom and live the life they want, no matter what their background, education, or money situation, it's just a lack of knowledge and action that has brought you to where you currently are today. This strategy is proven to do great things in a fairly short space of time. It's been amazing for me and my family. I've trained and mentored a lot of people over the years to get similar results as I'll share throughout this book.

I'm launching this book at one of the best times possible, just as the UK announced we have officially gone into a recession. Now you may think I'm crazy, but more millionaires are made during a recession than any other time. Why? Because many people are fearful and listen to the doom and gloom of the news, spewing out content about how there is a lack of money in the economy. This can lead to vendors becoming more motivated to sell and at a greater discount than if it was a buyer's market. Whether there's a recession or not, there is never a bad time to get into property development, it's just about buying the right piece of land for the right price, and if we can achieve this at the beginning, then we're already onto a life-changing profit from just one development.

Read this book without any distractions, with an open mind, and the belief that you can have anything you want, provided you are prepared to put the work in because life will be very different for you if you follow my step-by-step Property Developers Blueprint system.

CHAPTER ONE

Where it all Started

RETIREMENT AGED 19, WORKING 100+ HOURS A WEEK AND THE DAY
EVERYTHING CHANGED FOREVER

"Commit first, figure it out later" - **Grant Cardone.**

As I sit here writing this book on my laptop in the warm sunshine outside my bivvy, carp fishing in central France, with anticipation that one of my Delkim alarms could scream off at any point, sending the laptop flying into the lake, I'm deep in thought about what has worked, what hasn't worked, and the invaluable life lessons I've experienced over the past 35 years. These lessons have taken me from working 100+ hour work weeks to a life where I have gained financial freedom and choice.

This week's fishing holiday in France is just a small part of the 183 days a year I block out in my diary in advance, rather than trying to squeeze in a day here and there between jobs. The best part is, I don't even have to worry about the cost or loss of earnings while I'm away. The work gets done, in fact, more work gets done while I'm away than when I'm home. Squeezing in a holiday was rare in the past due to being constantly busy. Maybe some of you reading this book can relate to this?

Holidays now are non-negotiable. What goes into the diary gets done, and everything else revolves around it. So, why write a book while I'm away fishing? As I've said, what gets put into the diary gets done, and I saw this week as a great week away doing what I love, whilst using the opportunity to kill two birds with one stone.

It's peaceful around the lake, especially in the daytime when the sun gets too hot for the fish to feed. They would rather cruise around just under the surface or in the margins, soaking up the sun. It's the ideal place to sit and let the mind put what it knows into this book, a book I've been wanting to write for a long time, and one that is meant to help people make a change for a better life through property development.

I would be lying if I said I enjoyed learning at school, most likely due to subjects that bored me to death. Back then, I knew learning about Romeo and Juliet and History wasn't going to buy me a Lamborghini or the dream house - not that I was a car man at just 13. To me, school was just a laugh and one of my first achievements I gained was 'class clown,' which I took away with pride. School didn't motivate me one bit, and the teachers all wore tweed and walked around like robots. This was never a place I desired to spend more time in than I had to. Sixth form was a definite no-no, and University, well, that was never going to happen as I just saw this as a delay to get out working and earning some cash.

After signing in for registration each morning, I would always find a way to bunk off and go ride mopeds down the brickyards with my mate Steve. This was far more fun, even the crashes. School was just a waste of time that could be spent doing more enjoyable things like fishing and exploring abandoned buildings on my bike with my mates. Back then, I told myself the only way I could earn money was by using my hands as I didn't want to be stuck in an office, pushing paperwork around while the sun was shining - especially as we only got about 3 days of it in the UK. For me, I just had to keep my head down, wait for time to pass until I could get out there and earn some cash.

At 16 years old, I'd say that virtually no one really knows what they want to do with their whole life because up until then, we have spent it learning to speak, eat, spell, and walk. Most of this time at school is very controlled - what we wear, what time we have to be places, when we can speak and when we have to listen. An exam isn't to see how clever you are; it's to see if you paid attention because all the questions relate to what you've been taught. After school, the system simply spits us out into the real world and expects us to know enough to survive and in reality, it does just that - we just survive. Leaving school at 16 was supposed to be the end of education for me for life, or so I thought. More on this later.

My parents suggested that I get a trade. This was seen as a great achievement in our family, as no one had been one or self-employed, skilled at anything, a business owner, or gone to university. I initially thought about being a carpenter as I did actually enjoy the woodwork in school since you could see what you had done at the end of the day. I also enjoyed the metalwork and technical drawing. I learned later on in life that I am a visual person, which explains this. I tend to gauge my productivity and make decisions based on what I see, rather than the details I hear. However, becoming a carpenter went out of the window when my brother-in-law, who was a carpenter, came round to build a wall at my parents' house. I had seen him recently build my parents a conservatory which required expensive routers, circular saws, bench saws, drills, etc. I had inherited my dad's frugality and us Hubbards don't like to spend money. When my brother-in-law turned up to build the wall, he simply had a bucket of tools consisting of a trowel, lines, spirit level, jointer, soft brush, hammer and bolster. And that was the day that I dismissed the decision to become a carpenter and decided to become a bricklayer.

In order to gain an apprenticeship, you have to take an aptitude test at college. It is a 60-minute test to see how the brain works, and judging by some of the people taking the test, it was evident that their brains didn't work. Considering I had been getting "F's" in my exams from school, which I believe meant fantastic, I managed to score 99 out of 100 in the test. Even this shocked me, although I had found the test very easy.

My careers advisor suggested that I go for a site agent or project manager position since my score was too high to be wasted on a tradesman. I politely declined and made up my mind to become a bricklayer. At this stage, I did have options, as many people failed the aptitude test and their dreams of becoming electricians or plumbers were shattered in 60 minutes. They ended up becoming painters and decorators, which were seen as the bottom of the food chain in the hierarchy of trades. This was a valuable lesson to me, which I didn't quite realise at the time. The more you learn, the more you earn, as long as you take action. I do remember seeing my dad's disappointment that I had just walked away from a management job, but I knew I would be unhappy just sitting in an office all day. So I stuck to what I wanted to do, what would make me happy, something that a lot of people fail to do today due to peer pressure and the expensive world we live in.

With the decision made, I managed to secure a bricklaying apprenticeship at Peterborough City Council for the next 3 years. I would be attending Peterborough Regional College in several week-long blocks and day release, with the first 2 years focused on getting qualified and the 3rd year dedicated to gaining an advanced qualification. With most of my mates hating their time at college, I thought it was great, and I actually enjoyed the learning and practical side of things, far better than writing at school. I never missed a day and enjoyed laying bricks there. Some of the modules we had to build were quite technical, but I found it all fairly easy.

I soon found out the Council doesn't build; they just repair and do maintenance, so a big bricklaying job for me may be a couple of hundred bricks; anything bigger goes out to subcontractors on a price. What I did spend most of my time doing was plastering, roofing, tiling, etc, so I soon became multi-trade. This served me well throughout life as it allowed me not to have to rely on other trades. Sometimes you only need a plumber for 10 minutes to maybe move or cap off a pipe, and when you can do this yourself, you can soon save yourself quite a bit of money and not have delays on your jobs waiting for the trades to turn up.

The downside is you can soon become a very busy fool doing everything yourself, which was me in a nutshell. There was nothing I couldn't do. I could install a boiler, rewire a house, fit the kitchens, etc. The frustrating part here for me was not doing all of the work. As it was nice to do a variety of work, it was the fact that when I did carry out the work in the other trades like plastering and plumbing, my work was usually better than the people who were qualified and trained in that trade. I even had better tools than most of the other trades doing their own work. My Dad used to buy cheap tools from the market and Wicks, and they just don't do the job the same, and they break easily. I soon learned this was a false economy and that if you buy the best things, such as tools, then the result is then down to your own skills. I've stuck to this with my bikes, climbing gear, fishing gear, golf clubs, etc, and it definitely makes a difference in performance and results.

What I did hate about working for the Council was some of the houses we worked in; they were grim, and you'd be wiping your feet on the way out, not on the way in. It shocked me how some people actually live in today's world in the UK, and I soon learned a lot about the different demographics. What made working at the Council even harder was most of the lads went to lay bricks in Germany and Ireland, and they were earning in excess of £1000 a week cash at 18 years old back in 1991, while I was on the huge sum of £29.50 a week.

I desperately wanted to leave my job many times as it was rubbish, but it was my first experience of a recession. All the lads at college were losing their jobs on site, apart from me and another lad employed by Wilmot Dixon. I was surprised how quickly the work all came to a halt, and this was due to the high interest rates applied to slam the brakes on people spending money. They went up to 15%, which was unsustainable. At this time, all I heard and knew about recessions was that they were bad for everyone financially.

This has since been flipped on its head, as my mentor explained that recessions can be great, usually the best time for buying, just not for selling. So now, we actually look forward to a recession because when everyone is selling and really motivated, we can usually buy land and property at the best prices. Recessions come and go and form part of the property cycle - something I learned about. It's not always something you can time exactly right, but there are usually telltale signs throughout the cycle, especially as we lead up to a recession. People tend to have the most money they've had, living standards are great, everything is affordable, it's easy to get finance, employment is at its highest, fuel is affordable, there's no bad news going on, and interest rates are typically low. When you see this, you know it's not going to last, and a recession will be coming soon.

When a recession hits, property prices usually drop due to lack of affordability and demand, job losses come in thousands, credit dries up, and food and goods go up in price because fuel prices rise. Interest rates also rise, and this is where you are best situated if you have cash because you have buying power. So, if there's one piece of advice I can give you, it is to spend time accumulating cash during the good times while everyone is spending, and you spend that money in the bad times when everyone is selling. A recession is the best time to buy cars, motorbikes, jet skis, caravans, villas, etc, because this is when everyone needs to sell all the things (liabilities) they could afford when the going was good but now they can't. As I write this book, and go through the final edit (February 2024), the UK has officially announced that it has gone into recession, so you know exactly what we will be focussing our time on - buying land.

Part of my success came from never missing a day of college, as those were the only days I actually got to lay any bricks. I was probably the only student who looked forward to being there; I saw it as a day to test and improve my skills. My tutor saw that I had a natural talent and a great attitude towards the trade, and therefore pushed me to compete in competitions around the UK. I won several competitions with ease, then went on to the Nationals. This was the final 12 people in the UK competing to go to the world championships in Australia. It was a 2-day build with tight tolerances from the judges. I managed to win 3rd place for best bricklayer in the country, not bad for someone who hardly laid bricks, especially considering that the others had all been working with their dads since a very early age and had years of experience.

One thing I did notice regularly while working at the Council was that a lot of people who worked there all their life retired at age 65 and dropped dead by 66 or 67. Maybe you notice this in your company or the industry that you work in? I also noticed the same pattern with some of the other big employers around Peterborough, such as Hotpoint, Perkins engines, and the brickyards. This was not something I aspired to do—working all my life, having retirement plans in place, only to not be around to enjoy any of them. I've learnt that if a person has no purpose in life, then there is no need for them to be on the planet. And to back this up, just look at an elderly person who dies; their partner dies not too far behind, sometimes within a matter of weeks. So with this in mind, my decision was made and I quit my job at age 19. I was not going to trade my time for money for

50+ years in a job I didn't enjoy, just to receive a fake gold watch and a year or two left to live. Let's just say my dad wasn't impressed when I told him I'd quit, but it was my choice, and I was now responsible for my own actions.

I decided to start working for myself as a builder where I could earn more money rather than limit myself to a set wage each week, plus I could have more time off as employment restricted me to only 4-5 weeks. I was always doing private jobs on weekends, like most tradespeople, and as I mentioned earlier, I was a hard worker and never turned down work to earn extra money. Within a matter of a few weeks, I was really busy with work. I was doing jobs like patios, walls, porches, and fencing around customers' houses. As I always did a good job and the work came from recommendations, I soon had a couple of months of work booked ahead and at a better rate than I was getting at the Council. Happy days. Being multitrade helped secure a lot of this work because once customers saw your work and knew what else you could do, they would almost be looking for jobs for you to do because once you were gone, they would have to wait several months to get you back. They also knew that the rates would increase as the demand for work increased, so best to keep me on a job now. Getting work through good recommendations is still the best source of work rather than advertising, as long as it's the type of work you want to do and you're not just saying yes to everything.

Busy at work, earning double to triple my Council salary, things were going great, so I decided to have a holiday to Tenerife with my mate Steve from school. This was my first time abroad for me as my parents didn't have much spare money to bring me and my twin sisters up. I was always that kid left back at school while everyone else went on trips, but I understood the situation and it was what it was. While I was away in Tenerife, I couldn't believe how nice the weather was, the warmth of the sun and the heat at night, it was so different from the usual blowing a gale, cold, damp, and grey conditions of the UK, and I live in the driest part of the country near Peterborough so we get the best of the crap weather, in reality. I was hooked and had gotten the bug for more holidays, so next was a snowboarding trip to Andorra where I fell in love with the mountains. Again, the weather was amazing, fresh in the mornings but hot and sunny all day with no wind. The hot chocolates were amazing, and it was so peaceful just being there, especially on a Monday morning knowing that everyone was sitting in the traffic, stressed out and trying to get to their jobs on time. This trip made me want more, a lot more, so it was time for action again. With a bucket list written of all the places I wanted to travel, I decided to go on holiday again as soon as possible. I liked traveling so much that I went on a 13-year holiday, more of a retirement in my opinion. I thought I would do everything I wanted to do now while I had my health, no kids or responsibilities, rather than wait until I was 65, if I even managed to live that long. I didn't know too many people who went off to do ski seasons or cycle for months on end in their late 60s, so it was time to get it done now. Work was always going to be there, but life wasn't. This is something I want you all to think about.

Being self-employed, we tend to say yes to everything in fear of having no work, so we end up being busy doing jobs we don't really want to be doing most of the time. In reality, you won't be out of work for long, and if you do get a week or two without any work, you can use that time wisely to travel, work on the bits in your business that you've been meaning to do for years, or just chill out at home and relax. Trust me when I say that work will always be there, but life won't. This is why Property Development ticks these boxes for me - I get to travel, earn more money than I need, and it gives me freedom through leverage. I have the mindset that there will always be land to buy, so I don't have to have the scarcity mindset keeping me busy like most people.

The next 13 years were spent climbing the highest mountains all over the world. I travelled to the Himalayas, South America, New Zealand, parts of Africa, the USA, and spent several long summers in the Alps. I did many cycle trips all over the world on the touring bike and mountain bike. I did a whole ski season in a motorhome to 36 resorts. I lived in my van or tent for months on end. It was amazing how much I could do on such little money compared to my mates. I could do 3-4 months on the same amount of money they would spend to have 2 weeks all-inclusive in Majorca once a year. I know which one I prefer.

In order to fund this lavish tent lifestyle where I was having more holidays than Judith Chalmers, I would return back to the UK with one intention - to earn enough money to get back out of there. I would come back, ring up my mates, and do some site work on a price. My existing customers were always waiting for my return with a list of jobs like extensions and conversions. I also used to work for a few developers, building houses with my own bricklaying gang on price work. I used to enjoy this as you just put your tools in the van at 4.30pm, go home, and switch off, rather than spending every evening and weekends visiting customers' houses, looking at jobs and quoting. Half of the jobs you don't get, and customers are just getting prices to play against their preferred builder who will be working for peanuts. Site work was a better way to fund my traveling lifestyle for sure. It seemed that most developers would drive around to visit their sites in big Range Rovers and spend a lot of time on holiday in nice locations while the work was getting done by others. What an amazing life that would be, wouldn't it? What is strange is that most people never question how people make their money, and in this case, it was obvious: getting everyone else to do the work while the developer takes the profit.

I also worked for many of the big house builders with my bricklaying gang. This was pretty good work because we were quick and made good money from putting in the effort. We would often be the last gang standing if work slowed down because they didn't want to lose us. Remember to always spend time building a good reputation and demonstrating a good work ethic, and then you'll never be out of work.

I also built lots of commercial buildings such as supermarkets, power stations, and large industrial units. I liked this kind of work because I was always learning new things and was amazed at how these large jobs could be managed. Obviously, there was a whole team of people in the offices supporting the site agent, but it still relied on that one person on-site every day to deliver the projects on time. You could earn good money on these projects too, as they were commercial, not residential, and there seemed to be more money because it was a business paying for the development. Money never seemed to be a problem when it meant getting something built on time and open for business because of the huge penalty clauses in the contracts. Some of the supermarkets had a £100,000 a day penalty clause if a developer didn't finish the project on time. It was a good place to get materials for private jobs on the weekends, that's for sure.

If I returned to the UK just for a few days rather than a couple of weeks, I would sometimes do agency work, which is the easiest bricklaying work ever. I once had 5 labourers to myself, and I was just bricking up doorways on a new Asda in Wisbech. I used to get complained at by the other agency bricklayers for going too fast because I made them look bad, but I found it so hard to go slow. I'm a hard worker and I like seeing the progress we made at the end of the day. Instead of repeatedly returning to the UK to earn money and then leaving again, I made the decision to work abroad. Initially, when I applied, I was informed that I couldn't choose a specific location, so there was a chance I could have been placed in Paris or even worse, near Calais, for 9 months. Fortunately, I ended up being posted in Tuscany and the Mediterranean islands. It's important to always focus on positive outcomes, as this will bring them to fruition. Over the next few years, I set up tents and repaired caravans all across Europe. I worked in various countries including France, Spain, Italy, Austria, Switzerland,

Germany, and of course, the breathtaking islands like Corsica, Sardinia, and Elba. It was a dream job to work in such lovely weather and stunning surroundings every day, all while getting paid. This is exactly how work should be - doing what you love, regardless of the pay. Although it wasn't the highest paying job, earning only £97 a week, it didn't bother me, especially compared to those dreaded Monday mornings that everyone despised. Walking away from higher paying bricklaying work, which could earn me £700 or more per week, was quite easy for me, although some of my friends found it crazy. I knew that work would always be available whenever I decided to return.

There comes a point in life where one needs to mature and take on responsibilities. This was a message that my sisters constantly reminded me of. They would often ask, "When are you going to settle down?" My typical response would be, "Do you mean getting an expensive mortgage and watching soap operas every night?" That's what settling down looked like to me whenever I saw everyone back in the UK.

In 2004, I finally made the decision to take on some responsibilities. I was in a relationship with Sam again, along with her two sons, Luke and Lewis. It was time for me to leave the park home I had been living in for several years and buy our first place - a spacious three-bedroom bungalow on a large plot of land. However, this place needed some work, and being a builder, I submitted plans for three large extensions, a garage conversion, a conservatory, and a double garage with an annex. Why build so much? Simply because we could, and we ended up doing it. I'm sure many tradespeople reading this can relate, but just because we can do something doesn't necessarily mean we should. There's nothing wrong with using your skills to increase the value of your home tax-free, but it takes away time that could and should be spent on your business or wealth-building strategies, such as property development.

Before taking on these responsibilities, I hadn't had much income, likely due to taking over 40 weeks of unpaid holiday each year. Back in 2004, it was possible to simply sign a mortgage application stating that you didn't earn enough money but could afford the monthly payments. This type of mortgage was known as a self-certification mortgage.

A huge recession was hitting the world hard and just two days after we moved in, the self-certification way of doing things simply disappeared overnight because the money that was being lent out over the years as subprime mortgages, couldn't be paid back and it was having huge knock-on effects. This was leading to significant negative consequences. So now I had a multi-6-figure mortgage for the first time in life and zero work. This meant that in 2 years' time, I wouldn't be able to pay the loan back or self-certify again. This taught me a very valuable lesson: not to believe things would keep going forever. Recessions are cyclical, and there are good times and bad times depending on what you are doing. I've also learnt to not to react to big changes too quickly, especially with fear, as many changes are just temporary and will gradually recede back to the norm or not far off.

This has been seen recently with the government saying that all petrol and diesel cars will stop being produced by the year 2023. This doesn't mean they will be banned, just not produced. So this meant many people reacted emotionally and rushed out and bought a rather expensive electric car. Everyone has 8 years to go, but people panic and don't want to be left behind. I'm sure the government know what they are doing when they send these fearmongering messages out. As usual, the government has now backtracked and said 2035 now, which will most likely move to 2040 nearer the time as they know the infrastructure cannot cope with everyone going electric. Electric cars are now plummeting, and no one wants to take them in as part exchange because what garage owner is going to issue a warranty where they will be liable to replace a battery costing £20,000 or more. This is just a prime example of how the government waits for enough people to pile in on something that sounds great, then they move the goalposts. Either get in and out early, or don't get into it in the first place because you'll get screwed.

We eventually built all of the extensions, and Sam said we should sell and decrease our mortgage to take away a lot of pressure on me. After all, it was our largest outgoing each month, and it would make a difference. The housing market was still bad, but things were moving slowly. So, we put the bungalow up for sale, which sold pretty quick, then moved into a large 4-bed detached house. Me being me, decided to bang another 110m2 extension on it and completely refurbish the whole house, which took another 2 and a half years. I was also busy working for customers again, which meant all the work on the house had to happen in the evenings and weekends. The time had come to have a well-earned family holiday, so we packed the van up and went camping at Lake Annecy in France and then Lake Garda in Italy. I was feeling and looking worn out from working long days by the time I got on holiday. Sam asked me why I was feeling fed up. I had plenty of work, the mortgage was less than half of the other one, and the money was coming in regularly from work. I said that work just felt constant, it never stops. I'm always doing so many different jobs and never get to enjoy time off. She asked me what I enjoy doing, and I said garage conversion work — knocking walls out, building studwork, plaster boarding, etc. She then asked what work would pay me the most money, to which I replied, "garage conversions." Sam then said that garage conversions should be what I do then. Decision made, and the company was set up while we were in France, with a list of things to work on as soon as we got back to the UK. But for now, I would enjoy the holiday with the family.

Picking a niche like garage conversions worked great in a recession because people were struggling to remortgage to release equity out of their house for an extension or loft conversion due to stricter lending and a drop in house values. Being busy at work and doing the house all on my own was stressful and slow. Sam said she would never move again after this one was finished due to not spending time as a family, which I understood. Here I am working all the hours there is to provide a nice home and things for my family, but if you don't have a relationship with your partner or bond with your kids, then what's the point in doing it?

It was sign off day, and Stuart from Building Control was there signing off the house. While he was there, the phone rang. It was my wife Sam. "Did the house pass the inspection?" she said. "Of course it's passed," I replied. To which she replied, "I've been thinking…"

She said one more move would fulfil get rid of the £90,000 mortgage we had, which was tiny compared to the previous one. At this point, I had explained to her that I wanted to get myself educated in property and go back and see a couple of mentors that we saw in London back in 2009.

We had bought several rental properties with the proceeds from the sale of my mobile home and refurbished them, putting tenants in place and generating monthly cash flow. At that time, it was easy to obtain a mortgage with no proof of income, known as self-certification mortgages. We were also engaged in a few no-money-down deals, acquiring properties and having surplus mortgage money in the bank for renovations and other expenses. Despite being occupied with managing the house and working, I still managed to purchase a property every month. The reason I wanted to visit the mentors was that the method we had been using to buy properties was no longer viable due to the 2008/2009 recession, which forced us to halt our purchases. However, the other individuals seemed to be purchasing more properties than ever, suggesting that they knew something I didn't. When we left the event in London, I was already implementing what they were doing, so I didn't enrol in their sales training and mentoring. In retrospect, considering the seven years I spent renovating our own homes, what was the opportunity cost of walking away? It would have equated to millions of pounds in property and incredible monthly cash flow, to the point where I wouldn't have needed to work anymore. Talk about learning a valuable life lesson, albeit an expensive one. However, you can't control or change the past, only what you do next, right?

So we relocated again, resulting in us being mortgage-free at the young age of 40. This was one of the goals I had written down just two years prior after reading a book by Brian Tracey. At the time, I didn't realise the power of writing down goals compared to keeping them in my head along with all the other thoughts and distractions.

Being mortgage-free is fantastic, but it's just one monthly bill among many others, such as the growing appetites of our twin boys who manage to empty the entire fridge every 2-3 days. It took another two years to fully renovate our current home, all while living in it. We removed the floors, knocked down numerous walls and the chimney breast, replastered, rewired, replumbed, and replaced everything. I did most of this work myself after finishing my day job. It was exhausting. The garage conversion business kept me extremely busy, as it was now my sole focus. No more extensions, kitchens, or bathrooms - just this one type of work, which was much better because I could turn down jobs that I would have previously taken on. I had a few regular subcontractors who worked for me, enabling us to complete a garage conversion in just 3 and a half days. Our best week saw us completing three garage conversions, which was quite an achievement. When you work 80-100+ hour work weeks, things will eventually catch up with you. You'll often be too busy to notice, but other people do. You certainly don't have the time or the energy to go to the gym. Your kids are in bed when you leave for work and in bed by the time you get home. Your relationships tend to be text messages rather than quality time together. I'm sure many of you can relate to this.

Here's an exercise you should do right now: Add up how many hours you actually work, including commuting to and from work, visiting customers, quotes, fetching materials, paying and chasing invoices, emails, phone calls, social media, etc. Now divide what you earn a week by that number of hours, and you'll see your actual hourly rate. It's usually a shocker and remember this is before your expenses and tax are taken out. People are probably getting paid more for sitting at the checkout at Aldi than you are, and they get paid holidays, sick pay, and a pension topped up by their employer.

The big wake-up call for me was falling asleep at the wheel driving home from work, not just once, but on more than one occasion. One minute you're awake, then the next you're skidding into the field. Luckily, on all the occasions I skidded off the road, I managed to reverse my van back out and get home okay. Where I live in the fens, there are loads of drainage ditches at the sides of the roads, which are often full of water, and it was only a matter of time before I would end up in there, or worse, possibly hitting an innocent driver head-on. Something had to change, and it needed to be right now.

The house was finally done, and I was now booked onto a free 3-day event about property investing. I was about to learn from the 2 guys that kept on going while I had stopped. Sam had said I could go once we moved into the new house, but I knew I wouldn't be able to give the property 100% commitment if I was busy at work and doing up the house at the same time. These 3 days had been a long time coming for me. The day before the free event, Sam said she was busy and wasn't that bothered about going. For me, I was also really busy, and the event started on a Friday. This meant losing a day's pay, which was around £200 at the time. So, the little voice in my head was talking to me, reminding me that I'm too busy to take a day off, you're doing okay for yourself, it's going to cost you £200 just to go, you can go to the next one, and so on. But in this case, I stuck to what I said I was going to do. I had waited too long, and it wasn't going to wait any longer. So here I am with my wife, taking my first day off work in years, sitting in a seminar room surrounded by lots of strangers, thinking this is way out of my comfort zone. But if I learn just one thing, then it has to be worth attending. If the seminar isn't any good, we can simply leave during the break and I can be back at work salvaging the day's pay.

What actually happened was the first speaker came on and started talking about a few things I'd never really thought about much, but they hit me hard. Things like trading my time for money, which explained why I could never be wealthy, as we only have so many hours in the day.

"What is your why?" This confused me at first, but then I realised, this is what makes you get out of bed every day and do the things you do, even if you don't like it or want to. Financial freedom, time with family, charity, helping others, quitting the job, owning the dream house, luxury holidays, and high-performance cars were just some of the answers from the audience. For me, my 'why' was my family, freedom, and money. This is why I had previously worked so hard on things I didn't really want to do.

The speakers were also talking about earning money, big money, and this certainly expanded my thinking. I would have been happy working 60 hours a week part-time and earning another £10,000 a year. But they were talking 6 and 7 figures, which I couldn't imagine earning at this point.

Leverage was another concept being mentioned many times over the 3 days, explaining that one person can only do so much and that you need to leverage other people's time and money so it frees you up to do the things you enjoy. Every speaker who was having success used leverage, something I had certainly struggled with by doing everything on my own for years.

Multiple streams of income were also mentioned, and that really made sense to me, as I'm not one for putting all my eggs in one basket in case they break. I was already doing this by building a cash-flowing portfolio of properties that would go up in value over time, while working in my garage conversion business.

Then the word "Legacy" came up. Again, it was one of those words that I didn't really know what it meant. Legacy is what people would say about you when you're gone, plus what you'll leave behind, be that good or destructive. It's certainly something you should think about, not just in business. It's worth writing down what your legacy currently looks like and what you want your legacy to look like. I teach and mentor a lot of people, including my sons, in property development, meaning they can build lots of much-needed quality homes for people to live in. We provide people with lots of work, buy lots of materials, do online courses, raise a lot of money for charity, and have social media channels set up like YouTube that will live on and provide information long after I'm gone.

Throughout the three days, there were different speakers offering their training courses for a relatively small fee. This was great because you could spend three days learning from someone who has been there and done what you want to do, so you can fast track your journey without making the mistakes they made. Now, remember, I walked away many years ago thinking I could do this on my own, and to some degree, I had. But I had definitely been doing things wrong and nowhere near as quickly as I should have. So, the credit card got some action that weekend, and we signed up for quite a few courses. At this time, I wasn't really sure what I wanted to do, but I could see that all the different property strategies worked and that I was looking for one to replace my income and free up my time. I signed up on the basis that if I could learn just one thing that would help me, then it would be worth the investment alone.

It was nearing the end of the three days, and Sam and I hadn't really slept much because we were blown away by all the lightbulb moments and the training we had to look forward to. It was a strange feeling that we'd never experienced before, but we knew we were in the right place at the right time, doing the right thing with the right people. There was no going back now, and we were all in.

The final presenter came onto the stage. By this time, some people had left because the training wasn't for them. I wondered if they would be back in nine years' time with regrets like I was. The speaker was talking about something called a retreat in the Cayman Islands. My wife asked, "What's that?" I replied, "That's for the top people who have been in property for years." She said, "Why aren't you going on that, then?" I said, "No, it's for the top people and it costs a lot of money." I didn't even know how much, but it sounded expensive, and they had saved the best for last. They wouldn't give the price from the stage during the presentation, so that confirmed to me that it was going to be expensive. By now, we had already put £25,000 on my credit card over the 3 days, which was now glowing red hot. I was expecting a call from Mastercard at any point to check in on me and see if I was feeling okay, as I very rarely ever used it. All the other courses you could just go to the back of the room, pay, and book on, but the retreat was application form only. The application forms were handed out, and you had to answer 3 reasons why you think you should attend. I let Sam fill it out, as I wasn't spending any more money. As soon as the form was done, Sam ran to the desk and handed it in, telling the lady that "my husband is going on that retreat." To which the lady replied, "We'll have to see if his application is approved first." To which my wife just gave her the threatening look that said don't even go there, he's going. When she sat down, I had a moan at her, "Why did you do that? I'm not paying any more money, and they won't pick me anyway." Sam replied, "If that retreat is going to get you off the tools, I get my husband back, and the boys get their dad back. Then you are going on it, and that's final." And that was that. I was put in my place. 6 of us went for the interview, and 4 were awarded the place on the retreat, with me being one of them. I was shocked, as one of the other guys had far more experience than me, but it really did come down to why you wanted to attend. I never did find out the 3 things my wife wrote on that form, but they definitely worked.

The retreat was amazing. It was the first time that Sam and I had taken time out of our busy lives and truly thought about what was important to us, and more importantly, how we wanted to spend our time. We had been working so hard for far too long, and it was time for that to change. The other people attending the retreat had all been in property and business for a good few years, and we soon realised that we were the least educated and definitely the poorest. I soon learned that these are the exact environments and people to be hanging around. If you're the most intelligent and wealthiest person in the room, then you're in the wrong room, and you cannot grow, which makes sense, right? Being around this small group of like-minded people was incredible. They would all offer great advice and support from their years of trial and errors in business and the wins they had achieved. They certainly made you realise that becoming a millionaire was possible within a few years of working on the right strategies with the right support.

Putting pen to paper and writing things down makes a huge difference rather than it just floating around in your head. My mentors would advise on the strategies required to get me to a certain income, create a roadmap with whom I needed to make it happen and what to expect along the way. Just like having a start and a finish destination in a sat nav, you follow the instructions and you get to where you want to be. Getting away to an inspirational place every year without the day-to-day distractions is essential for everyone who wants to grow a business and create a lifestyle of freedom and choice. I always say you cannot do this at home on your own at the kitchen table on a wet weekend in Peterborough, it just won't happen.

We have been running our own legacy retreats for small groups of people every year since 2017. Many of the people return year after year because with growth comes new challenges and ideas that we stress test, then create a new roadmap and goals for the year ahead. Maybe you're ready to work out where you really want to go in business and life and attend a retreat? Maybe you have a business you want to grow, launch, or sell, or you are just at a crossroads in life and don't know which direction to take? You can see what a retreat can do for you on the link below.

www.developinghomes.co.uk/retreat

There's no denying that the past 8 years have been a rollercoaster of emotions, challenges, and wins, but the past 4 have been incredible. All the hard work and persistence does pay off, and everything that we've focused on has happened, not by luck but by the plans we made year on year. Why have the last 4 years been different? Well, my ex-business partners thought they would be greedy and help themselves, so they took everything from me within just 1 hour, including the money in the business bank account. I was left with nothing, not even an email address. It was like I hadn't existed for 2 years. Why has this helped me succeed? Because when you have nothing, you have nothing to lose, and it was down to me to pick myself up and get on with things.

One of the greatest things I've learned is that you can lose everything, but they can't take away your knowledge or mindset. If you have that, you can come back quicker the next time around. You can take everything from me today, and I'll get it all back and much more quickly than before, and that is a powerful place to be, rather than one of fear. Many successful entrepreneurs have bounced back after losing everything. People like Donald Trump, George Foreman, Steve Jobs, 50 Cent, and Gerald Ratner have all made a greater comeback after the setback, so never let starting from where you currently are in life be a reason not to succeed.

Summary

1. Schools teach you to follow the system. Don't spend your life doing a job, career, business, or work that you don't enjoy. You're only on the planet for a very short time, especially with your full health.

2. Know what your true values are, what is most important to you, and live by them daily. Your gut is the brain that you need to listen to when making any decisions; never go against this, as you'll pay the price later on.

3. The more you learn, the more you earn. Never stop learning and improving your education and personal development. Become the very best version of yourself possible, as this will rub off on the people you surround yourself with, especially your kids.

4. Recessions can actually be great for business, especially for buying land at a cheaper price. Observe the masses: when everyone is selling in a recession, it's the time for you to buy cheap land, then sell the houses when the economy returns - which it always does as demonstrated by the property cycle.

5. Grant Cardone once said, *"Commit first and figure it out later."* Saying yes to opportunities instead of overthinking has allowed me to excel. There is no growth in your comfort zone, so get comfortable with being uncomfortable.

6. A black book of contacts can be worth millions of pounds, get you what you want, and connect you with the right people who can open doors for you. I leveraged my mentor's black book of contacts. Your network really is your net worth.

7. What you say yes and no to has a huge effect on the outcome of

your life. Saying no can sometimes be the quickest way to success, rather than saying yes to everything and becoming a busy fool.

8. Investing in yourself is the best investment you can make. Delay buying the stuff you don't need and work on yourself daily. Everything you want will come as a result of that investment over time.

9. Retreats can be truly life-changing. Taking time out of your busy life to really think about what you want to do is the difference between success and failure. All successful people have a vision and goals, so they know what to work on. Opportunities are passing us by daily, and only once you have a clear plan do these opportunities appear and make the vision a reality.

10. No one gets a second chance at life. The countdown clock is ticking from the second we are born. Start creating the life you dream of right now, rather than keep saying one day, someday, maybe, or when you retire.

CHAPTER TWO

Why Property Developments?

"The only way to do great work is to love what you do" **- Steve Jobs.**

Something has drawn you to this book to learn about property development, so I believe it is really important to look at the strategy in depth, not just the lifestyle that it can create for you, but the pros and cons as there are always both.

First, you need to know if this strategy is going to get you where you want to be. As we've discussed in the previous chapter, hardly anyone knows really where they want to be because they are too busy working and only thinking about a month or so in advance. Asking yourself really important questions like these can make a big difference in getting started and achieving what you really want.

Do you want an office? If so, how big?

Do you want to employ people? If so, who and how many?

Do you want to be hands-on or hands-off?

Do you want to go big and do huge sites?

Do you want to just work 5-7 months a year and take winters off?

Do you want to project manage or use a main contractor?

Do you want to just build bungalows?

Do you want to build locally or nationally?

Do you want to build to sell or build to rent?

Do you want to start building one house or more on your first build?

There are a lot of questions that we run through on our retreats to figure out these answers, not just in developments but in all areas such as family, health, charity, legacy, holidays, hobbies, wealth, you, and business. There are lots of important things to look at when making these and other decisions.

Property development is a chunky money strategy, and what I mean by that is it delivers large sums of money as profits towards or at the end of a development depending on how many units you build. Receiving large sums of money in one go will usually mean you need an accountant who can arrange your tax affairs to suit your goals because you don't want to be paying the taxman more than what you need to. You need to retain as much of the money that you earn as possible. For instance (as a family of 4), we can earn over £300,000 a year tax-free through our development business. That's £75,000 a person a year tax-free. Now compare that with someone earning £75,000 as an employee. They would be paying £21,696.60 in tax per year. Do this over a 50-year period, and that's £1,098.480 just in tax alone. I don't know about you, but I know I'd rather have that £1m in my pocket than go to the taxman for them to waste. Running a lot of expenses in what you do through your business will reduce the amount of money you need to take out personally and therefore reduce the amount of tax you pay.

Many won't be able to or want to wait until the end of a development to get paid, which is understandable. But here's one of the best reasons that I love property development: it is possible to pay yourself £4000+ a month to manage your own developments. Yes, you can pay yourself a decent wage to run your own developments. Lenders, which we'll talk more about in the funding section, encourage you to pay yourself to be fully invested in the project. This is like getting paid some of your profit upfront but as monthly cash flow. This may allow someone to quit their job or stop working for customers straight away and then be able to give 100% of their time and energy into the project. To a lender, this is better than someone who works 60+ hour work weeks and the development is seen almost as a side hustle. As much as you only need to spend 5-7 hours a week on a development, the lender wants to know that the project is being run on time and on budget.

You'll be pleased to know we never make less than £100,000 from any development (one house), and as much as many of you would be happy with less than this, especially on your first deal, I'd always advise you not to drop much below this because you don't need to. Most people will ideally want to be able to go full-time in developing once you get paid from that first development, unless you live off the project manager's fee.

The average size profit on the development sites from the people I mentor is around £450,000 - £500,000 on their first deal, so they are aiming for a good-sized profit to springboard them into developments full time and escape their existing work. Just imagine what that could do for you if that amount of money landed in your bank today? Write down the things you would buy or do because if you don't know what you would do with the money, then the brain doesn't have the same desire or motivation to work for it, especially when things seem difficult or hard work. With the average salary in the UK being around £33,000, £450,000 could pay off your mortgage, pay down your debts, have that dream family holiday, maybe work seasonal like we do, buy the dream car. Maybe the car can wait until development 2 with delayed gratification, but it is an extremely useful exercise to see what difference this amount of money can make to your life.

After being a busy builder for many years and trying many other property strategies, property development really fits in with my values, which are time, freedom, and money. I can leverage other trades to do the work while I spend time doing what I like, such as going on holidays, playing golf, and fishing. When I was a busy tradesman, I found I was always so busy looking at jobs, working on the tools, fetching materials, quoting, paying bills, and so on that I didn't have much time left to do enjoyable things. These things are what make you the person you are. With developments, I spend less than 30 minutes a day managing things on our sites, usually at different stages all at once. Buying a site, building a site out, and sales on another site don't take up much time, and believe it or not, it's easier to manage building five houses than running two to three small jobs around customers' houses.

I also have the freedom to work when I want, which is why we spend the winters abroad in the sun or skiing, while working on things like planning, legals, utilities, etc. We then come back to the UK to start the sites around April when the days are longer and the weather is nicer. Summertime on site is so much more productive due to the weather, not to mention the morale on site. When the sun is shining and the sites are dry, the trades really enjoy being at work. Come wintertime when everything is damp, cold, windy, and everywhere is muddy, people would just rather be somewhere else, especially as their wages drop that time of year also due to lost wet weather and shorter working days.

Then, of course, there's the money. Being able to live a pretty good lifestyle doing what I want when I want, while having more tax-free money left in the bank at the end of the year than what I spend, to me, this is the dream business.

In today's busy world, demand for housing has never been greater than it is today, and the challenge is that there is no solution anywhere in sight, not even a slow one. We're living longer, more people are migrating to live in the UK, and fewer migrants are leaving. This is fundamental in building a successful business. You can have the best product in the world, but if no one needs it, then the business will fail. Note I said, 'needs' it, not 'wants' it. There is a huge difference, and everyone needs food, water, and a roof over their head.

Back in 2008, the housing crash was huge, and the government clearly showed during the time of Covid in 2020 that they were not going to stagnate the housing market again, even while we are going through a recession. During Covid, construction workers were allowed to continue going to work, planning laws were greatly relaxed, and some new permitted development rights were implemented very quickly. This shows that the government is supporting developers regardless of the property cycle; they need us to fix the problem they've caused by not providing enough housing. I don't know of any other industry like this that gets the push and support from the government, especially when economic times are not the best.

Some of the biggest problems in supplying enough housing, apart from the slow planning process, are the aging workforce. I retired from site work at the age of 32, and apart from the odd labourer who didn't last long, I was the youngest person ever on site. Most people were in their 50s to mid-50s but looked and worked more like they were in their 70s. The years of manually handling heavy materials, working outside in all weathers, definitely take their toll, and by the time they get to that age, it's really hard to do anything else or learn new skills.

One thing a recession does is force a lot of people out of the construction industry as they get laid off. They then go and get driving jobs or work in factories, which can pay good money, but for most of the guys, it's also the first time they will be paying into a pension and have a company contribute. The age hits them as this is one of the first times they get to reflect on their current position. They'll also experience things like paid holidays and working in the warm and dry, so they very rarely return to site once things pick up, which as we know, they always do.

Something that is a real shame is the lack of young trades coming into construction. I don't believe this is for a lack of people wanting to but more a lack of opportunities available. Most people working on a construction site will be working on price work, so they don't have the time to stop doing what they are doing to teach young people the skills they require to work. How can we expect anyone to take on an apprentice for 3-4 years with such an uncertain economy from a broken government? No one has any reassurance that next year will be a good one, so no one commits to growing their businesses.

My twin boys are 21 years old and very skilled for their age. They quit their plumbing and electrical apprenticeship after just 1 year to do developments because they could see their bosses always working long hours and phones constantly ringing because they were working in a reactive business. Now, this also used to be me, working crazy hours for customers with the phone constantly ringing, but as I started doing my own developments, I started to get my time back and did things like playing golf while the bricklayers laid the bricks. My sons soon saw the difference in me and preferred developing as a career rather than being a busy tradesman for the next 45+ years like their bosses. I'm glad they both realised this at their age rather than spend the next 30, 40, or 50+ years working in the wrong career while hoping for different results.

Some people label the youngsters as lazy and useless, but there is definitely some amazing talent out there that is being wasted, so I do encourage everyone reading this book to give someone a go, a chance to prove themselves. Take them under your wing and give them some responsibility; they may just shine, and you could be responsible for guiding that person onto an amazing life with good skills and work ethic. I've done this many times with some of my son's mates. They come to work on our sites, I show them how to do things, get them on the tools, and I become their labourer. It really is amazing how quickly they can pick things up when they are given a chance.

I'm currently in the process of buying my boys their own site for them to work on, run, and manage. It's a single 3-bed bungalow traditionally built, where they should make around £100,000 - £110,000 profit for 5 months' work as they will get paid the labour for the trades they do and the developer profit. They will do about 80% of the work such as the foundations, the brickwork, the roof trusses, tile the roof, the plumbing, the plaster boarding, the groundworks, and all of the landscaping, which they are more than capable of. They will improve existing skills and learn new ones. If I'm not away on holiday, then I'll be there laying a few bricks and blocks with them, enjoying the sun, the radio on, and of course, a bit of site banter.

Over the past 14 years, I've done quite a few other property strategies prior to doing developments. None of them come anywhere near when it comes to making money and not taking too much time up. I'm not saying that none of these other property strategies don't work or that money cannot be made from them, but developments far outweigh any of the other cash flowing strategies, and here are a few main reasons why.

Buy-to-let (BTL)

Buy-to-let properties typically require a substantial deposit (25%) and a BTL mortgage (75%), which will have a far higher interest rate compared to your own home. Owning property in your own name as opposed to a company comes with different tax implications, especially capital gains tax made on the profits if you were to sell in the future. In 2023, the government reduced the amount of CGT relief, meaning you pay more tax. I can see there being no CGT relief on second properties in the future because many people own them, and the government would make millions in tax overnight. The worst thing is that there is nothing you or I can do about it, just like the other tax changes. Most people will run out of deposit funds once they buy 2-3 properties because they leave their deposits locked in for years. Then they start doing joint ventures, meaning they halve their profits and have to do double the number of properties to get the same returns as doing them on their own.

Properties do go up in value, but do they really? What I mean by this is that a property may double in value every 15-20 years, just like everything else we buy. Therefore, it has more to do with going up with inflation rather than being extra money you receive. What you can buy for £10,000 today will cost you £20,000 in 15-20 years for the same thing due to inflation.

I personally don't think waiting for property to go up in value is the best strategy because who wants to wait 20-30 or 40-50 years to reap the benefits (which will be heavily taxed once you decide to sell)? The government decided that mortgage interest could no longer be offset, meaning that if you take £10,000 a year in rent payments from a single property, then all of it would be classed as income rather than the £3,000 you make after deducting the £7,000 a year mortgage expense. Add this to your personal tax, and it could push you into a higher tax rate, making it more costly to own BTLs than make profit on them.

Typically, you'll make around £250-£350 profit per calendar month before any tax, maintenance, voids, council tax, and the mortgage to pay, tenants not paying rent, boiler breakdowns, accountancy fees, insurance, agency fees, etc. Ask yourself this, how many of these BTLs would you need to own to live a half-decent lifestyle? The answer is lots, a lot more than you probably thought, and by then, you've created yourself a full-time job managing properties and tenants. Is this the dream job? You'll also need to factor in the fees when you keep renewing a mortgage every 2-5 years. They are usually a few thousand and can be added to the loan, which decreases capital growth gains. I've been spending the past 2 years selling all my BTLs off as they gradually become empty. I can make far more money from the equity by using it in developments and without the hassle of managing many properties and tenants.

Houses of multiple occupancy (HMOs)

This is where you buy a normal house and convert the house into individual rooms with en-suites, then rent the individual rooms out instead of the whole house. Now these can be much more lucrative for cash flow because instead of having one tenancy agreement in place, you can have multiple agreements. We usually have six per house. So first, you usually have to do quite a major refurbishment, which costs money upfront and takes time. One thing I often see is that people can take months and months doing these conversions, and they forget that every week a property isn't rented out means no rent is coming in, so time is definitely money. Finding good builders can be hard, both to get a price quote and to do the work sensibly because of a loose description of the work that needs to be done. So you get budget overruns, delays in the build, and a loss of rent. This isn't everyone who does HMOs, but it is certainly the majority, as the construction part is the part you need to get right.

Over the years, HMOs have become very popular because many people like to live in them since their bills are all included in the weekly rent payment, and they can use what's left for their own purposes. Our tenants tend to be migrant field workers or food produce workers. Brexit did see a bit of a wobble for a brief period with a lack of tenants, as some did return to their home countries. However, the UK desperately needs migrant workers, and if they don't come from the UK, they will come from other countries around the world. Some landlords just stick to professional workers or trades working away on large construction projects who have higher expectations than migrant workers, so understanding your market is key.

We've discussed how the government allows a scheme that is good to happen for a while, then once lots of people take advantage, they then move the goalposts. Well, the government has started charging council tax to each en-suite room in some areas around the UK, with more councils getting involved on a monthly basis. This can seriously impact your cash flow, possibly reducing it to zero in some cases. I've seen this a lot, where the strategy seems saturated and when enough people are involved, they bring in regulations and tax changes knowing it's going to cost people to stay in or get out. It soon restricts new people from entering the market as well.

With HMOs far outweighing BTLs in terms of cash flow, you can see why many turn to them since you're buying a property with a deposit anyway, so you might as well buy one that pays out significantly more per month. Once you have too many HMOs in an area, it can become a race to the bottom in business as landlords lower their room rates just to cover their expenses or have to spend money on high-end rooms because tenants have plenty of choices in where to live.

HMO properties will be harder to sell if you decide to exit the market because you'll usually have to convert them back to a normal dwelling, which takes time and money. Additionally, you'll still have to pay the mortgage and council taxes for the number of rooms you have.

One last thing is that a lot of lenders don't like HMOs, and the ones that do charge a premium on the mortgage interest rates compared to BTLs because they are more difficult to manage. One great benefit of an HMO that I like is that if a room is empty, the remaining rooms usually bring in enough money to support it, meaning you might still make a profit or at least break even.

Serviced accommodation (SA)

This is now a hugely popular strategy where you take a property, fully furnish it, and rent it out per night using platforms like Airbnb and Booking.com. These can provide good cash flow, but they have a high turnover of people, so there is more cleaning and maintenance involved. Additionally, the booking fees can be 15%, which can have a big impact on your proceeds after the mortgage. People like serviced accommodation because they can add their own personal touches to the interior design, rather than opting for a boring old vanilla BTL. However, you can't control who stays in your property, so they can often be used for sex work or stag and hen parties, which may not be your ideal clients.

Knowing your market is key, and some people stick to holiday lets or construction workers who work away and aren't in the property much. Setting up and furnishing a property to a high standard can come with substantial costs, as there is usually no shortage of competition. With competition, you are continually decreasing your profits by having to provide more quality at your own expense, or by reducing your rates, which decreases profit. Either way, competitive markets are usually not the most profitable, so it becomes a race to the bottom.

A big issue I've seen many times is when someone manages to acquire 2-3 properties and their turnover hits the VAT threshold. This instantly takes an additional 20% off their turnover in VAT, which is usually their maximum profit. As a result, they end up running the additional serviced accommodations at break-even. This is something that I haven't seen taught on training courses because why would they? Credit card fraud is fairly common and on the rise, especially with last-minute bookings. This is where most of the fraud occurs, so you could end up letting your properties out to strangers and not getting paid. It's definitely something to be wary of.

Rent to Rent (R2R)

This can be a great strategy for anyone who doesn't have much money. It involves agreeing on guaranteed rent with a landlord who may have had enough of managing their own properties and dealing with tenants. You agree to take over the property in full, then you tenant it either in an HMO or SA-style tenancy. This is definitely a numbers game. There will be some setup costs to get going, but a big benefit is that you don't have to take out a mortgage so you can do unlimited amounts of these, even if you have a bad credit rating. The downside is that you don't own the property, so you don't gain from the capital growth. Plus, the landlords can take them back either by using the break clause in your contract, which is typically 6 months, or after a few years of the agreement, meaning your cash flow is never guaranteed.

Either way you do it with R2R into SA or HMOs, you will be a very busy landlord, and you will need a lot of properties to have a good lifestyle. Could you do one development in a far shorter period of time and gain from one big chunk of money that sets you free?

Deal packaging (DP)

This is where you find properties for sale or direct to the vendor, agree to buy the properties usually at a slight discount, then find investors who want to buy those properties. The investors are usually cash rich but time poor, such as dentists, doctors, lawyers, etc. Typically, a sourcing fee would be payable, around £3000. Now, the training courses out there will tell you that you can package up a deal once a month every month to replace your salary, but there is no way you will be packaging a deal up bang on the 28th of each month and getting the cash in your bank, so there could be some longer gaps between your fees.

For investors, it's usually about timing and getting the right properties at the right price in a specific area, so piecing all this together can be tricky, and that's if the investor is still there once you get everything in place. I've seen many investors pull out at the very last minute for many reasons (or excuses), meaning that you have to find another investor immediately, or you end up letting the vendor down who has put their faith in you to help them move on. It is a bit of a chicken and egg strategy: do you find the deals first or investors first? Either way, you could be doing the same amount of work packaging land deals up but for far greater profits. More on this later.

Refurbs (Sometimes known as flips)

This can be a great place to start because you should get all your deposit out and your profit to go again. Most people aim for a £25k - £50k profit, which is okay if everything works out and you get the full asking price. But what if the market drops 10% or there are more properties than buyers, meaning they have more choice and negotiations? Ultimately, you still have to find a property that you can add value to by giving it a full refurb, so why not spend the same time looking for a plot with planning? You may have to add a large extension, loft conversion, or major alterations to add that value - these all add up and take time. Most new builds will have a 24-26 week build program to completion, and I've seen many people take 1-2 years to do a basic refurb because they try to do it themselves and figure it out as they go. Probate properties are usually the best to buy, but with people living longer and agents having their preferred buyers, it can be hard to find them on the open market.

Commercial Conversions (CC)

I've done a few of these, whereby you take a building, usually a commercial building such as pubs, offices, or solicitors, and convert it into habitable dwellings. There are some great permitted development uses with commercial buildings, meaning the planning process can be cheaper and quicker. The downside I see is working out what they are going to cost to convert, which can be tricky, especially for a beginner. You are usually ripping out a lot of the building before you start putting it back together, and structural alterations can be expensive and time-consuming - this is very different from a new build that is predictable. Lenders are not that keen on you reducing the property's value while you do the strip out, so they tend to loan less money, which means you are putting in far more money at the beginning.

Finding a contractor to quote for the work can also be tricky as they will factor in a lot of the work that may not be straightforward because you are altering a building that was never designed to be lived in. Just the insulation, soundproofing, and fire prevention can add up to huge amounts on some of these old commercial buildings. Once you start going above 3 floors, a lift will need to be installed, otherwise buyers won't be interested - and these will have to be maintained and managed even once you sell the properties.

The largest one I've done is an office to 34 apartments, and when you do conversions on this scale, the thing that catches a lot of people out is that all 34 apartments have to be completed before any occupancy because of fire risk. And who wants to live in a building under construction? So trying to time 34 buyers to all move in at the same time is impossible, which means the sales process takes a very long time. With developments, we would simply do phases of 6-10 houses at a time, meaning you can pay down some of the finance as you go, which increases profits, rather than having the maximum loan sitting there for months on end while your builder finishes off and snags all of the rooms before the sign off and habitation can complete.

New build (NB)

Now I may sound biased on this one, but remember I've done all of the other strategies, and for me, this is the clear winner by a mile. New builds are very predictable on costs with labour and materials. Labour usually works on prices set by the market, so bricklayers get paid the amount per 1000 bricks, carpenters get paid by hanging each door, etc. You shouldn't really go over budget when doing a development.

You will usually have a scheduled program to follow, so you know exactly who is needed, at what point, and in the right sequence. You will know exactly how long they should take before they've even done the work, which is very easy for you to manage because you have a program to follow, and you can organise things weeks in advance.

I project manage my own developments, typically spending 15 - 30 minutes a day max sending a few emails or WhatsApp messages to my trades and suppliers. Keeping good communication is key to a project running smoothly. Some of you may like to go down the main contractor route whereby someone else runs and manages the whole project? I chose to do this on the 34 apartments I built as the site was nearly 3 hours away. Apart from the upfront work to get started on site led mostly by my architect, it would usually consist of a once-a-month site visit and a spot of lunch to check on progress before driving home in the Range Rover.

Which do you think is more desirable, a brand new house all modern and ready to move in or an old house that needs some work due to it being personalised from the previous owners? New builds always sell, even in a slow market. Think about what choice there is for home buyers, it will either be the large housing estates by the big developers, or the houses that we, the small developer builds. Our property will always sell far quicker because most buyers only have the option of a 3-story townhouse, no privacy, small garages, no parking, and tiny gardens, whereas we build bigger garages, open plan living, better quality fittings and 3-5 houses is a good, sweet spot as there aren't many for sale like this.

Now, I've given you an insight into some of the other strategies, there are a few more golden reasons that developments are amazing.

Overheads, the noose round the neck of many businesses and even more so in a recession. With a development company, we only have the setting up of that company, usually limited, and that costs around £15, done online and takes minutes to do. My accountant then charges me a flat fee of £1000+ VAT, regardless of whether that company does £300,000 turnover or £2m. And that's it, no office, no staff, no plant, and no vehicles although I do have a van (for fishing). This means starting a development business is virtually free as you'll pay your accountant later on. Just a laptop and a phone, which is a business expense. Most businesses go and get £000's in overheads before they've even taken a penny, which doesn't make good business sense to me. Keep things as efficient as possible, then if you take the winter's off like we do, you're not paying out £000's of pounds a month in overheads or having to take on work just to keep people employed.

One of the things I see many builders fall foul of is when their VAT bill is due, they haven't put any money away and this can ruin their business from bad money management. This is why many stay under the VAT threshold of £85,000 because they don't want to manage it plus they think charging an extra 20% will lose them work. My accountant told me it's the exact opposite and that breaking the VAT threshold is actually a sign of success because you now have unlimited earning potential. You can't earn £100,000 a year if your turnover is less than £85,000, can you?!

Do you get a big VAT bill that always seems a pain to pay and the wrong timing? With developments, we actually get a VAT rebate as new builds are exempt, some of these rebates can be £20k - £30k a month which really helps with cash flow. Just imagine getting a check back each month from HMRC rather than a big bill once a year that you have to pay almost immediately or they charge you interest?

With developments, it is very scalable. It doesn't take twice as long to build twice as many houses. You can simply bring in 2 or 3 of each trade who, as we've mentioned, will work on fixed prices so it won't cost any more money to build bigger or faster. We're quite happy on a rinse and repeat strategy, building 1-5 units a year and taking the winters off abroad. Bigger sites would affect this and it means you have to sell more houses to get to your profits.

When I mentor people, I always tell them that it's good to have a plan B. With developments, there are several exit strategies, such as build to sell, which is what we do. But there is also build to rent, where you build the houses, refinance with a mortgage, and then rent the properties out, creating cash flow. Or you can build for the housing associations, either as a Joint Venture partner or build and then rent them back on a long-term repairing lease. This is a much better way of becoming a landlord, as they are almost doing a Rent to Rent with you, where they tenant and manage the properties for 10+ years. They either refurbish the properties before handing them back, or they renew the lease and go again because they would have to evict and relocate all the existing tenants. It's best to know this at the outset, so you build the right types of houses which we'll talk about in the next chapter.

Modern Methods of Construction (MMC) are here, and while they do have their challenges, which we'll discuss, they do provide an amazing solution. MMC is where certain parts or even the whole building can be constructed off-site while the groundworks are being done. This means you can build far quicker rather than building the traditional way.

I've been to quite a few of the factories and seen the houses being built and installed. Seeing two houses built on site and completed within six and a half hours is beyond impressive, especially when you consider that there are zero snags, the defects from trades work that usually someone has to pick up and be paid to correct. The modules, as they are called, are built in a dry environment in a large factory, then transported on lorries to the site, which are then craned into place. Other systems are panelised, such as timber, steel frame, and polystyrene formwork. All of these systems reduce the labour and management on-site, so for anyone wanting to run and manage their own sites, these systems are definitely worth looking at. If you follow me on social media, you will see that I use timber frame a lot. This saves us considerable time on-site, which results in greater profits and getting the properties to the market sooner. With the fully volumetric system, you only need two contractors, a groundworker, and a factory, so management really is at a minimum.

While many of the cash flowing strategies are okay, you have to ask yourself if £250 a month going into your bank really makes a difference to your life, or will £100,000? In my opinion, it doesn't take much more effort to build a house than to do one up. You still have to find the land, get it through legals, pay for it, and sell it, so you may as well make a life-changing profit than just a few hundred quid.

As you can see, there are a huge number of benefits with developments, many of which I'll be sharing as we go through the next chapters, but the ultimate one is that property development is a system and systems can be learned. After looking at all the developments I've done, I've noticed there are eight simple steps to take in a 1-8 sequence, meaning you can't just start at step 6, for example, and get things wrong. These eight steps have been proven to deliver amazing profits time after time, and as I currently go through the purchase of my son's site, we are still following this exact same system today.

The good thing is you and anyone else can follow the same system one step at a time and make the money you desire to give you a life of freedom, profit, and choice. It doesn't matter if you have money or not, are skilled or not, or are experienced or not, as I've trained and mentored hundreds of people to follow the system and get amazing results. I'll be sharing some case studies later in this book so you can see that we have many different types of people from all walks of life achieving life-changing results, and you can too.

I've called this system the Property Developers Blueprint, and hopefully, by you reading this book and taking the necessary action, this will be the day you look back on where everything changed for you. You can go out there and get the life you truly deserve, living a life on your terms where you have options to do what you want, when you want, with whomever you want, as much as you want to. So let's get started on step 1 of the Property Developers Blueprint right now.

Summary

1. All property strategies work, but most will make you busy and create a job for you rather than give you freedom.

2. Just one deal can be life-changing with property developments. £100,000+ makes a difference to nearly everyone's life, whereas £250 per month doesn't.

3. It's possible to get paid every month to run your own developments, meaning you can quit your job sooner.

4. You only need to commit 5-7 hours a week to property development; it's not a full-time business unless you want it to be.

5. Property developments allow you to work seasonally, take the winters off, and get on-site in the spring and summer when the weather and morale are much better.

6. The demand for new housing is huge and is not going to be solved anytime soon. Property development is a less crowded strategy, and there is always less competition at the top.

7. Property developments have hardly any overheads, which keeps you streamlined compared to most businesses that have high running costs per month.

8. Modern methods of construction are here; embrace this technology rather than being left behind like HMV was to iTunes and Blockbuster was to Netflix.

9. You can pay little to no tax through property developments. You want to keep more of what you earn; most other strategies will tax you heavily.

10. With property developments, you can get a VAT rebate each month instead of a large VAT bill. This will help you with cash flow throughout the build.

CHAPTER THREE

Finding the Land

"If something is important enough, you do it even if the odds are not in your favour"
- Elon Musk.

Before we start, let's get one thing clear. There is an abundance of land around us at all times. In fact, only 1.4% of the land in the UK has been built on to date. This includes housing, schools, shops, offices, warehouses, and hospitals. So now that we have an abundance mindset, we can get to work on finding our first building plot.

Instead of just rushing out and buying any old piece of land that we see for sale, we need to first identify our goldmine area. What I mean by this is finding the sweet spot where there are deals at the right price, the demand is there, and there are plenty of amenities that tick the boxes of the buyers. Without these 3 things, we could simply be buying the wrong piece of land, and that's the main thing we want to avoid in step 1.

Let's look at Peterborough as an example, a city where I was born with an estimated population of 216,300. There are affluent parts in Peterborough where you can go for a walk, and it's a nice place to live, and like most cities, there are other parts where you wouldn't dare go for a walk, even in the daytime, as it resembles the Bronx in New York. There's also a very different price bracket from, say, the Welland estate to that in Longthorpe, which means a very different demographic lives there; one has more renters, and the other has more homeowners.

You should divide your town, city, or village where you live into 4 quadrants and give a rating from 1-10 on where the best but affordable places are to live; you'll probably rule out 50% of your circle location straight away. Then look at no more than a 1-hour radius from that quadrant as we prefer to build in the villages that are like satellites around the town. The reason I advise not traveling more than one hour is that you will visit the site regularly, even if you have a main contractor, and most likely daily if you are managing and working on your own sites, so you don't want to be spending hours and hours driving as this can be non-productive time and time away from your family. Also, there's a good chance that the further you go, the less you will know about the area. Sticking to one area allows you to become known, build your brand, build your power team, and get the deals coming to you. More on this later. I've personally stayed away from building in busy towns; the land is expensive, you'll build smaller properties, and it can be a nightmare to organise materials and labour in and out of sites. Trades also don't like working in busy places very much because the parking is usually a nightmare, and they get stuck in traffic every morning and evening. Just think of the tools they need to get in and out of their vans every day, and you can see why.

We generally focus on building two types of properties: 3-5 bedroom detached houses and 3-5 bedroom bungalows. There are more buyers in this price bracket. When looking at our goldmine area, we look closely at things like commuting to and from work for families, being close to schools with good Ofsted reports, and whether they are near a supermarket or shops.

With the bungalows, our buyers are more interested in being close to places like the doctors, the bus route, and a convenience shop, whereas families require parking for 2-4 cars. We also look to build properties in a location that we could rent out if we decided to switch strategy or if the market changes, a plan B if you like. As much as it would be nice to build the £2m Grand design houses, you will be limited on the number of buyers, even more so with the number of renters.

So with our goldmine area set, buyers will be looking at what amenities are available. The world is changing rapidly, especially since Covid, where people think, work, and live very differently. This will most likely include you and me also. One of the things we always design in our family homes is a study now, as many work from home that would have gone to an office beforehand. It's nice to have a dedicated work zone where work gets done and you can close the door on it at the end of the day, rather than having to clear the dining table as the kids come home at 3.30pm for dinner after school and the chaos begins. We've also started to build most houses with open plan living, which is really popular as families like to be together rather than in separate rooms. This usually includes the kitchen, dining area, and a lounge or sunroom as they are often called. We'll often include a separate lounge if the parents want somewhere quiet to retreat to, or they can be used as a playroom where the parents can simply shut the door and leave all the toys everywhere but out of sight. If you've got kids and stood on a piece of Lego, do you know how much of a selling feature this is?

Now that we've identified our sweet spot, we need to start looking at different ways to find the land, as there are plenty. In fact, we have over 30 different ways. We'll touch on a few of these in this chapter, but I would advise you to choose three main ways to find land that you enjoy and can become good at those three rather than trying to do 30+ and dilute yourself too thinly.

We buy most of our land on Rightmove. People are shocked when we tell them this because their natural response is that all land on Rightmove is overpriced or there must be something wrong with it. In most cases, they would be right. But if everyone talks like that (and believe me, most do), then surely this creates an opportunity for us because they are ignoring Rightmove? Here lies a valuable lesson in life: what we actually say to ourselves. Is it positive, negative, factually correct, or are we labelling everything the same, such as all estate agents are rubbish? They can't all be rubbish, so this is not factually correct. However, we can soon catch ourselves labelling them all that way and therefore fail to build relationships. In this case, we must say to ourselves that Rightmove can offer us some amazing land opportunities once we do our due diligence further.

Some of the land that does end up on Rightmove for sale may have issues, such as contamination or archaeology, no different than off-market land. Rather than walking away from land with issues, we need to understand that the masses have already talked themselves out of the opportunity, leaving fewer buyers. Problems can usually be resolved over time and with money, sometimes a lot of money. But these costs are simply just reflected in the offer price and used to our advantage. More on this later.

The good thing about Rightmove is that it's a very easy platform to use, especially for a beginner. You can simply scroll through land and properties quickly and set parameters, such as price and distance. We set the search distance to 20 miles from our house because we don't really want to travel further than this. 20 miles one way could take you down a very busy road into town, meaning a 1-hour drive, and 20 miles the other way could see you traffic-free through the countryside with the journey done in 30 minutes. So again, you can filter out which part of the radius to concentrate in. It is always worth looking in the perimeter 20-30 miles because you could be missing out on a few opportunities at mile 21-23, which you would be more than happy to work in if a deal came up. It's just best to search within that 20 miles first to see what is available.

For your first site, it pays to start small, get your developer experience. Then, if you want to scale up on the size of the site or rinse and repeat, you can do so. We like sites of 3-5 units. Again, we find they are the sweet spot to build within 8 months so we can get away abroad for the winters. Plus, they tend to sell really well, as 2-4 neighbours is like a small community where everyone will get to know each other and feel safe, rather than a big estate. The buyers like doing the neighbourly thing, like putting the bins out, taking a parcel in, or keeping an eye on the property while they are away. Safety in numbers, as they say.

We usually look for sites with outline planning. We'll talk about this in one of the other steps later, but it's where I advise you to start so you de-risk yourselves and can get started on site much quicker than a site with no planning. As much as we take sites through to full planning from the start, we also still like to buy a site with outline planning, which gives us certainty and can allow us to get on with the build.

Concentrating on making that first life-changing sum is key, and I've seen a lot of people spend years and thousands of pounds stuck in the planning process, only to do nothing in the meantime and miss out on £000's of pounds. While they're spending this time trying to get out of their jobs, we are doing several developments and making some great six-figure profits, not forgetting the months we spend away as a family. So outline planning, no more than one hour away from home, is the best place for you to get started.

Viewings are essential, and if it's just a parcel of land, then the agents will usually say, "Just have a drive out and let me know your thoughts." They don't usually meet you on-site. Whereas, if it's a garden plot which we like to buy often, you'll either meet the agent and most likely the vendor. Now, meeting the vendor, in my opinion, gives you a 90%+ more chance of doing a deal because people do business with people they know, like, and trust. If you make a great first impression, then you're over halfway there. We've built some great relationships with vendors and shook hands on deals within 15 minutes of meeting them. I always look that we'll be working next to a vendor's house for 15-18 months, taking into account the buying period, build, and sales period, so you need to make sure that you will get on.

If I'm with the agents or vendors on viewings, I'll always ask them if they've had any offers. Sometimes the agents will lie, but we can often see through their agents' talk. I'll also ask them what's the lowest price they will accept on their land, and most will give you a price there and then. This can save a lot of back and forth with the negotiations and at least give you a figure they would like to achieve. I've bought 99% of my plots below the lowest figure that they say they will accept, so we'll talk more about that in the offers section, but it is such a key question to ask. Seeing how long a site has been for sale can be a sign that the site is overpriced, the vendor isn't that motivated to sell, or it's probably fallen through a few times from previous buyers who couldn't get the funding in place, which is really common.

Meeting with estate agents is definitely going to be one of the great ways to get deals. At the beginning, you are going to be getting out there and doing the work by meeting them on viewings. But over time, as you build up relationships and rapport, they will start to bring you the deals, hopefully before they go out on the open market. Some of these will be deals that are coming back on the market, often at a reduced price. And at other times, they will be offered to you before they go back out to the market. We've bought several sites this way, and they are quite easy to get agreed at a great price very quickly.

Vendors like to work this way so their neighbours don't get to see an agent's board going up and selling their land, as they become jealous, knowing they are getting a huge sum of money for a bit of garden or grass. A big advantage here is that more often than not, there is only you on the scene for the first few days, maybe a week at most. With it being just you, it means you don't end up getting caught up in a bidding war with other buyers, thus driving up a price higher than you wished to pay. So off-market deals can be great, but you're most likely going to have to give it a good few months before these start coming your way.

To get started, I would go visit all of the estate agents within your goldmine area, one by one. It may be time-consuming, but it will pay off. You don't have to visit every single one in a day, but maybe 5-8 each day until you've been around all of them. All estate agents are different, and you need to go into a few before you find someone that you click with, someone who takes you seriously, someone who seems ambitious to bring you deals and get you deals at the price you've asked for. Once you have a couple of good estate agents, then keep them on your side, as they will eventually get out there and do the leg work for you. One mistake I see that a lot of people do, and it's definitely not going to be as productive, is that they just email the agents the lazy way for details rather than meet face to face. Meeting face to face is the best way to go, and remember, the masses are not doing this as they are too busy or just sending in the emails. Agents like to get out of their office, especially if it's a nice sunny day, and many of them get a small bonus for going on viewings, so get out there and get meeting them.

A question I often get asked is, *"Do estate agents take brown envelopes full of cash?"* Well, I personally don't think there's anything wrong with giving an agent an introducer's fee of, say, £2000 for a deal which completes and one on which you are going to make a six-figure profit. Without them, you wouldn't have gotten the deal, and by offering an introducer's fee, they will be incentivized to bring you even more deals. This is quite common across the industry, but some agents still frown upon it as a bribe, whereas we see it as a win-win-win. The vendor gets to sell and move on, we get to buy land that we will make a good profit on, and the estate agent gets a nice fee for introducing us. In reality, money talks and it makes the world go round, so bear the introducer's fee in mind, but spend a little time sussing the estate agent out before suggesting this.

There are typically two types of estate agents: residential agents and commercial agents. The latter definitely understand valuations and the commercial aspect, given that you are a business trying to make money. There are also two types of estate agents in that some are large and operate nationally, while others are small and independent, which could be just one shop or several in a single town or region. Some even operate purely online to reduce their overheads and, therefore, charge a much lower fee. This can entice the sellers in, but the agents don't always meet the vendors or do viewings, which means it can be harder to build rapport. I personally prefer the small independent agents, as they are more focused on customer satisfaction than sales, and it's their own business, so brown envelopes are usually welcomed with open arms.

There are lots of online portals specifically designed to search for land, both on and off the market. I like to use Google Earth because it's free; you just need to know what you are looking for and be able to keep track of the sites you are looking at. This method allows us to scan over the villages and see how large the garden plots are, or if there are overgrown infill parts. When we spot something with potential, we'll find out who owns the land and then send a letter to them, seeing if they are interested in selling. These can be great deals as there is only you and the vendor, so you cut out the middleman, the estate agent. Our current site of three bungalows was sourced using Google Earth and a targeted letter drop. One thing we spot regularly, and which is often a telltale sign that the vendor may sell, is a large trampoline. Kids grow up and then don't play in the gardens anymore, so selling the garden may be a better option.

This is one of my favourite three ways to do deals because you get to always speak directly to the vendor. There is also no misinterpretation between the agent telling you what you want to hear and the vendor telling them what they want to hear; it's just the two of you talking directly to each other.

You get to determine an agreed price, which is great because an agent will usually overinflate a land value because they often don't know how to value it in the first place. They usually inflate the land value to get the vendor onto their books, for which they will net a small fee in their pay packet. We will demonstrate to the vendor how we've arrived at our offer price, which can sometimes be below their expectations, but once we've built rapport and explained the offer, a deal is usually done very quickly.

Some vendors don't want their neighbours knowing they are selling their land, and the last thing they want is a huge estate agency *"For Sale"* board with lots of viewings going on or a *"Sold"* board. Money does strange things to friends and families, so many like to keep things quiet.

Word of mouth is something that people don't think of as a strategy, but it can be one of the very best. Telling everyone you know or meet what you are looking for works really well, and if someone doesn't know of anything straight away, then they might hear of something later on and think of you. I always tell my mentees to tell anyone who comes within 3ft of them what they do and what they are looking for. This can work for raising money (which we'll talk about later) or for finding land and contractors. The barbers or hairdressers is probably one of the best places for word of mouth because they know absolutely everyone, and they are the kings and queens of gossip. You could even offer to pay them an introducer's fee of £1000-£2000 on successful completion. This may make a significant impact to someone standing there cutting hair all day, and if you pay an introducer's fee, you can guarantee they will be looking to introduce you to more people.

A way that has become very popular in recent years is buying at an auction. This has come from the TV program *"Homes Under the Hammer."* Many a novice has bought something at auction that they didn't originally intend to buy but still made a few quid by accident. This may have worked well several years ago and in a rising market, but I only want you to buy the right deals that will always make you a significant profit, at least 6 figures. Many people have bought something without even looking through the legal pack or doing a viewing, something I highly recommend you don't skip past. Buying property can be easy to get in, but it's harder to get out, especially if you buy a dud. Someone joined my mentoring program after buying some land in an auction. They couldn't get planning on it and were struggling. I put them in touch with my planning consultant who told them that they would never get planning on there looking at the local planning policy. The mentee had to walk away from a £17,000 deposit plus auction fees. If he would have learned the Property Developers Blueprint first or came to me for advice and support, he could have saved a lot of money and done things correctly.

Before making a purchase at an auction, I'd always recommend just going and visiting a live auction house to see how everything works and what the properties and land sell for from the advertised guide price. Just remember to keep your hands in your pockets at all times because a scratch on the head could result in you buying a laundrette 250 miles away for £400,000.

What is becoming more popular are online auctions. These are great as you can watch from anywhere in the world as long as you have a phone signal or a Wi-Fi connection. The lots, as they are called, will have a low starting guide price to get interest up and start the bidding. Properties will usually sell around 25-30% more than the guide price depending on how low an auction house lists them. I've seen properties that would sell for £150,000 listed at £30,000 which, as you can imagine, gets a lot of interest and early bidding. This soon drops off once people know they are never going to buy it anywhere near the guide price.

Buying the later lots can work really well as many people will have already bought something, meaning fewer buyers in the room. You can always approach the auctioneer after the auction and ask them about the lots that didn't sell to see if the vendor will sell and you can strike a deal. As you can imagine, if a lot doesn't sell, then the vendor will be even more motivated than they were before the auction, knowing that you may be their one and only last chance to sell. One thing to note is that you will still be under auction conditions, meaning a 10% deposit payable on the day and completion within 56 days. So make sure everything is in place regarding your funds and power team.

You could buy deals from deal sourcers saving you time looking, but from my experience, there aren't many deal sourcers out there who really know what they are doing, and they will simply send you a link to have a look at without them doing any due diligence whatsoever. They will often say they have exclusivity on it, but this is often a lie, so it could sell through someone else at any time while you're spending time and money on the due diligence.

A deal sourcer typically charges 2-3% of the purchase price, which is fine as they may be bringing you an exclusive deal that no one else is offered, but I would be wanting these things in place as a minimum.

- A lock-out agreement or option agreement with the vendor.
- Ideally off-market, but if it's locked out, then that's fine. Just make sure the lock-out period covers you for how long it will take to purchase, which is typically 16 weeks. So a minimum of 20 would satisfy me better.
- A fixed price agreed with any conditions clearly stated.

- Planning in place or a breakdown of costs that are required to take it through to planning.

- A breakdown of recent sold house prices with backed-up data such as the last 3 months sold data on Rightmove or a RICS valuation.

- A breakdown of build costs, utilities, roads, etc.

Basically, the deal should be packaged up and agreed upon, ready to go for you. If it ticks all of the boxes and the due diligence is approved by your solicitor and lender, then it should be fine to proceed with confidence. Deal sourcers should get paid at the end of completion, so be warned of any asking for fees upfront as they won't be motivated to get you through to completion. It might be worth asking the deal sourcer for some testimonials or social proof to ensure they know what they are doing and provide a good service.

In a nutshell, every Council around the UK is under pressure to deliver a set amount of housing, and almost all have failed to hit their targets imposed by the Government anytime soon. They have 5, 10, and 20-year strategic plans mapped out, so it's not like they don't know where they will allow development to happen next. This creates a huge opportunity for small developers like us to get out there and take advantage of the land available to make those life-changing profits.

Summary

1. There is an abundance of land everywhere. With this mindset, we will have plenty of opportunity and not have a fixed mindset like the masses.

2. You need to identify your goldmine area first, where it works and where it doesn't so you are not fishing in the wrong pond.

3. Speaking directly to vendors will definitely improve your chances of securing a deal and getting a better price, rather than going through the middleman, the estate agent.

4. Building relationships with multiple estate agents is key. It will take time at the beginning, but going out face to face on viewings will help massively in the long run.

5. There are 30+ ways to find land; pick three and become an expert in those three strategies. Become known for what you do and finding deals this way so you attract the right types of deals you want.

6. Not all deals are overpriced or have problems on Rightmove like the masses think. Look at each deal on its own merit, then arrange a face-to-face meeting with the agent or the vendor directly.

7. Auctions can be great places to buy discounted land and property, but make sure you have everything in place ready to buy, and only buy what you came for.

8. Identify the amenities that your target market requires in your goldmine area. People are not just buying a property but also investing in things that help with their lives.

9. At first, you have to go out and put in the work looking for land. If you put the work in, then the deals will start coming to you, and some of these will be the deals that have fallen through or are off-market, which are the better deals to get.

10. Do not underestimate word of mouth. Telling everyone you meet within 3ft what you do can have a huge impact on opportunities brought to you for a small introducer's fee on successful deals completed.

CHAPTER FOUR

Assessing the Plots

"Once you decide to work for yourself, you never go back to working for someone else"
- Alan Sugar.

Once you've located your plots of land within your 1-hour radius from where you live, you're going to need to know what to look for so that you don't make the mistakes that many other developers make. But where do you start when you are just looking at a garden, an empty field, or in most cases, an overgrown jungle?

It comes down to looking at things that may restrict or make it difficult to get planning or issues that could arise later on down the line that can be very costly. This is definitely something we need to mitigate before we consider buying or even putting an offer in. One of the first things we will look at is the utilities. Is there gas, water, electric, drainage, and telecoms available? Because there's no point in building a house if you can't get these to the property, and even if you can access these services, you need to make sure they are affordable for the development to stack.

There are various services that you can use to see if the utilities are all nearby, but you need to check also to see if there is an adequate supply, especially if you are doing multiple units. Most infrastructure is outdated and at its maximum limit. Most houses these days require a 3-phase supply to be fitted which the developer installs and pays for. This is to allow for fast car charging rather than the overnight trickle charge available to most households. This can put a huge strain on the outdated network. This isn't a choice for the developer to make; it's part of the new building regulations that came in 2023, making it compulsory for every new dwelling to have a car charger installed. I think we will see more eco criteria enforced over the coming years, and the building regulations have recently increased the amount of insulation going into a property. You only need so much insulation before the properties can become too warm. I often drive past a site we built, and they have the windows open in the winter. So much for saving the planet.

Gas in new dwellings is being phased out in 2025, but the government being the government may have to move their unrealistic goalposts, just like they have done on the production of petrol and diesel cars. If we're doing a desktop appraisal, then we may just do a Google Street View to see if properties near the site have gas. As we build in a lot of surrounding villages, we don't take it for granted that gas is there. It really can be street or even down to a few houses, meaning you may have to pay for expensive connections or look at alternatives such as air source heat pumps, which again will cost more money. It's not uncommon for the houses on the outskirts to be on oil, electric, or tanked gas for heating as the villages expand over time.

When you look at a plot, you might see nothing but a flat field of grass or even a nice garden, but what is under the ground that you can't see? There could be a huge gas or water main, drainage pipes, or a culvert. These will be really expensive to divert, and that's if it's even possible, as they require a certain amount of room for a machine to be able to come in and carry out repairs in the worst-case scenario.

Utility companies make their money from diversions, not from new connections or attending repairs. I've seen many people go on to buy a plot of land with planning, yes with planning only to find out later that there is a main service running through the plot that makes the development unviable financially or not possible to build. These plots can often find their way into auction houses or hang around on the market for several years until one unlucky uneducated developer buys it thinking they have got an absolute bargain. My advice is if you look at any plot, always do your checks first.

Some of our sites come with Archaeology or contaminated ground. These things need to be looked at before buying the site as there can be significant costs associated with the issue. 90% of people will usually walk or run away from sites like this at a glance, whereas we actually see them as opportunities because there is less competition and they don't know how to resolve these issues.

These problems can usually be resolved, and they may just need to be factored in financially, or there could be alternative methods to reduce the work required to fix the problems. Either way, see to look at problems as your opportunities, and how you can be a problem solver. The vendor has a problem site that is not going away. They don't have a big queue of buyers lining up fighting over it, so this is where you can step in, buy the site at the right price, and allow the vendor to move on. Even if it's a £100,000 contamination problem, this would be factored into our costs and used in the negotiation process.

On one of our development sites, the contamination was set to cost £360,000, a huge amount that would almost make the scheme unviable, but with some of the changes I made and with my experience, we managed to get this down to around £12,000. That's an incredible difference and it was a lot less work also. I like to solve problems, and it's definitely one of my strengths. Many people choose to be mentored by me year on year so I can handhold them through their first site without making mistakes and help them negotiate a great win-win deal.

We've also had archaeology on a couple of our sites, and this costs less than most people think once you learn the process and what's actually required. Having to pay an archaeologist to stand there every day watching you dig out trenches scares people, but like I mentioned, and the same with the contamination, their costs are just factored into the deal and used as a negotiation tactic.

Many sites may come with a dwelling or buildings on them that need demolishing. An asbestos survey should be done on commercial buildings before they are open to the public, so make sure you ask for this, as it will show you where the asbestos is located. Once again, you can factor the work into your costs.

If there are existing buildings on the plot, then you may be able to save some money due to the services that may be connected, such as drainage, water, gas, and electricity. Some of the buildings may be able to be used for site huts, reducing your preliminary costs. However, from my experience, you're better off refurbishing the property and getting it back on the market than letting the workers sit in there. They can also be prone to arsonists and squatters, so you don't want to leave them sitting around empty for too long. A site cabin is a better option; they are not that expensive, and remember, time is money.

Each plot is usually registered, and you can see who owns it, when they purchased it, how much they paid for it, if they have a loan on it, and more importantly, if there are any restrictions, such as a 1 dwelling limit or an agricultural clause where you have to fit certain criteria to be able to live there. There are ways to get these restrictions removed when you have a solicitor who knows what they are doing. One person's problem makes 99% of people walk away. Solve the problem, and you can grab yourself a bargain.

If you're looking to build near or right next to existing dwellings, then you will need to look at a party wall agreement. You don't want to start excavating right next to a property and cause some damage, then end up in a huge and expensive lawsuit, so these definitely need to be put in place before you start any work. I mentor a lot of trades to become their own developers, and many of these have been doing building work and extensions without using a Party Wall Agreement. This is risky, and you certainly don't want to do this with developments. Neighbours can soon put a stop to the work if you don't have the agreement in place, causing delays and unnecessary expense. The reality is you don't know what you don't know, so it's best to learn this stuff so you do things right in the first place.

A lot of sites will have trees on them, and you may look at cutting them down to make way for new dwellings. Some of them are protected, meaning you can't just go cutting them down. There may be big consequences, such as huge fines and even imprisonment, so it's important to check first.

The planners are always looking to use someone new as their case study to show the high levels of punishment they can dish out. Please don't let this be you. Protected trees will be registered and listed, so the information is out there. One thing we look at when removing trees is where we pull out the large roots. This will leave the soil unstable, so it may interfere with our foundation design and add additional costs that need to be factored in.

For any trees that remain, and just as importantly, the ones in neighbouring plots, they may have an impact on your foundation design. These would need to be built to withstand future growth of roots and the changing ground conditions from rain. On our current site, we had to build raft foundations because next door had a small willow tree and another three neighbours had conifers. This had nothing to do with what was within our own plot, but it did cost several thousands of pounds more to install.

On another site, we had to put in a more expensive foundation due to building next to a sloped watercourse. This is why it's important to assess the plots, see what risks there are, and then factor in any associated costs into the deal before you offer and complete.

With the good old UK weather changing more times than a traffic light, rain is now causing more flooding in areas that have never experienced it before. This can lead to more expensive water attenuation systems and even cause damage with sinkholes caused by the water eroding stable ground.

Other things to look for underground can be old mine shafts, previous landfill sites, different makeup of ground types, water courses, old ponds, etc, so make sure you focus more on what is underground rather than what you see above the surface.

You can only see so much detail on a site from your phone or laptop, which is why it's so important to actually visit the site, even if it means having a look from the road before organising a viewing with an agent or the vendor. I've seen so many things while out on site visits that can cause big issues, such as asbestos covered over (some on purpose), huge tree roots covered by long grass and bushes, cesspits, old wells, and old fuel barrels that have rusted and leaked into the ground.

Usually, I'll visit a site with my wife or sons so that one of us is talking to the agent, while the other is having a walk around checking on things. Just make sure you take some wellies as the sites can be wet in the summer with long grass.

It's very easy for an agent or vendor to distract you from looking at any issues there may be on the land. A second viewing can always be great because you see and notice so much more. The amount of houses and land that we've bought, completed, and then picked up the keys, only to get inside the property and things look completely different, especially once the furniture has been removed and the garages emptied. It can sometimes feel that the vendors have swapped the boiler for something 10 years older and the carpets.

As you know, we prefer to speak to the vendor, and if the first visit is with the agent, we'll usually pass by and knock on the door to try to speak to the vendor directly to ask some more questions. Just make sure they're not having their dinner when you knock, as they'll be less receptive.

By now, you know there are many things to look for when looking at a plot of land. We use a checklist so we don't miss anything off because just one thing could cost you thousands or cause lengthy delays on the site later on. This checklist also allows us to take notes that we can look back on for future reference or action steps to take to derisk the site because you will soon forget this after looking at so many sites.

Photographs and videos are always a great way to keep for reference later. It's worth creating a spreadsheet to keep track of all of the plots you look at with the address, date visited, notes, pros/cons, offer price, etc. Ideally, you should be looking at 10 sites per month, and the more you look at, the better you will become at spotting any issues, asking the right questions, or carrying out the right due diligence without committing lots of money before offering on a piece of land.

Summary

1. Visiting a site in person is essential to see what risks there could be above the ground.

2. The bigger risks are usually underground, not what you see on the surface. Ensure you do the correct checks and never assume.

3. Problems can be opportunities, so be careful what you say to yourself because you could be saying the same as the 99% who walked away from a life-changing deal.

4. Having a spreadsheet to track all of the plots you look at for future reference keeps all the information in one place.

5. Visit in pairs so one can talk to the agent or vendor while the other person walks round and takes notes, photos, and videos.

6. Make sure you check for utilities in the ground. Often, land is not built on because of main services running through the site.

7. Never assume you can just cut down trees; they may be protected, and any trees you do remove may have implications with the ground stability.

8. Make sure you note if a party wall agreement is required. Don't rely on your contractor to do this, and make sure it's in place before any work commences.

9. Always aim to meet the vendor, even if it means doing viewings in the evenings or on weekends. You are 90% more likely to do a deal this way.

10. Look into the history of the plot: what was it used for? Has it been built on before? Are there any risks from years ago that could cause problems?

CHAPTER FIVE

Planning Permission

"You don't have to be great to start, but you have to start to be great" - **Zig Ziglar.**

As we discussed earlier in this book, it is advisable for you to start with a plot that comes with outline planning permission as a minimum. Planning is all about risk versus reward, and some of the most profitable developments we have done have gone through the whole planning process from the very beginning, and at some point, you will too.

While many people fear planning permission being refused, let's remind ourselves that the country is short of 4.3 million homes. Yes, 4.3 million. So we know that this problem isn't going to get fixed anytime soon, and the planning process is just part of this bottleneck. Only 234,000 houses were built in 2022-2023, which was known as a boom year and construction was flat out. Even when the going is good, it can't deliver the minimum of 300,000 homes that the Government set as its target. 2024 is set to be a slow year as the recession starts to bite. Construction started slowing down in the Autumn of 2023 when the interest rates started to significantly affect home buyers' affordability. I say slowing down, but many sites came to a complete standstill and laid everyone off. Every council in the UK is under huge pressure to approve developments and try to ease this gap, but with an archaic planning system, they have an uphill battle ahead.

Taking a plot from the initial consultation with your architect to submitting planning and getting everything approved and ready to put a shovel in the ground can often take a minimum of 9 months, and this is if everything goes through without any issues. Then you have another 6 months to build the house and 4 months to complete the sale. This is why nothing will ever be fixed because everything takes far too long.

So if planning takes this long, what is happening during all this time? At the outset, you may speak to your architect about what they think you could build on the land. They may have submitted many applications and have a high success rate as they understand the planning policy, or they may have good relationships in the planning office where they can simply have a conversation with a planning officer for guidance. Ultimately, the application needs to be submitted and validated, which can take ages, and then it goes out to the public for consultation. This is where the delays begin.

Ultimately, you need to build what the market demands and what the planners will approve according to the planning policy framework, so don't worry too much about getting personally involved. Architects should design development schemes with the developers' build costs in mind, but not many do. Many architects are simply designers and can soon add lots of fancy stone arches, fascias, and soffits, complicated roof designs, and request that expensive materials are used because they are designers, not developers, and they want their names to be recognised for awards, which brings in more work. This simply won't happen with them designing a 3-bedroom square house with an up-and-over roof.

We often strip out some of the things that other architects have drawn when we buy the land. This is known as value engineering, where you reduce the build costs to make the development more viable or profitable while still providing quality and value. We can save tens of thousands of pounds by value engineering, making more schemes viable and profitable that otherwise would be too expensive to build.

If you're looking to obtain planning in rural areas or in town locations, a planning consultant could be a good person to have on your power team for advice. Planning consultants understand planning policy and have many tricks up their sleeves to get your sites through planning that the council may otherwise refuse. A planning consultant can always give a brief to your architect at the beginning, so they design a scheme from day 1 that will have a high chance of approval because it ticks the planning policy boxes.

Whether you use an architect, planning consultant, or both, they will all look at many factors required by the planning department, such as whether the site will put a strain on local services like doctors, schools, and hospitals. Many councils charge a Community Infrastructure Levy (CIL) on developments to help pay towards these services and the creation of new ones. As much as this levy can make some schemes unviable, I do think it is fair that a developer contributes something towards improvements if they are to build many new homes in the area.

CIL does need to be urgently looked at by the council because it can usually be absorbed in larger schemes, but not when building just 1 house. Some councils even charge it on home extensions which, in my opinion, doesn't really put any more strain on the services. If anything, this creates more jobs, which pays more tax and gives people a better place to live.

Another fee that may be payable is the Section 106 (S106), whereby the developer contributes towards affordable housing. This can be done in a number of ways, such as 1 in 3 houses at 90% of their value once you build over 10 houses. Some councils are 1 in 3 regardless of how many you build, so you need to check your area. You can offset the S106 houses by contributing sums of money to the council, but this is on a case-by-case basis and depends on what the council needs more urgently: housing or money. The S106 does expire with the planning, so if a vendor has spent a lot of money, time, and stress to get something through planning and the agent has overpriced it, then if the planning is running out, they may be more motivated to drop the price or work together so you can retain the planning and the S106, rather than having to go through the whole process and cost all over again.

Planning fees can soon add up, especially on multiple units, and one of the councils near me doesn't allow you to have another submission for free anymore if they refuse the application. This could be refused simply because your architect didn't include the right fee or missed something off. Do you think councils will be refusing more applications if they can get paid twice? Absolutely, which will go on to cause more delays and expense.

One way to de-risk an application is to do a pre-app, either at the beginning or if you are looking to make significant changes to an existing scheme. This is where you can submit a pre application for advice from the planners on the likelihood of the scheme getting approval. Pre-apps can be just a form sent in, or they can be done face to face in some council offices or even out on site. Some councils are free, and some you have to pay a fee for, so check out what your council offers and if there are any costs. The pre-app isn't approval, but it's advice on steering you to submit the right application, and I've seen cases refused even on a planning officer's advice, so there certainly is no guarantee in planning being granted. It does allow you to test the water for free or very little money and without risk. I also look at the pre-apps as a way to meet with the planning officers face to face, build some rapport, let them get to know you, and see how proactive they are towards development. Once you get to know your planning officers and they get to know you, things will always be quicker and smoother.

If we buy land without any planning permission, we will usually lock the vendor into the deal, whereby we don't pay anything unless we are successful with planning, and if we don't get planning permission, we can resubmit or simply walk away without being stuck with some land we can't get planning on.

This strategy works really well as you only have to put in a small amount of fees as your risk money, or entrance fee as I like to call it. Before we get into one of these deals, we will always speak to our architect and planning consultant about the likelihood of planning success or knockback. If it's a 60% plus chance of getting planning approved, then we're happy to go for it and commit. The vendor can sell the land, but we have the agreement in place to buy it, still subject to us gaining planning. So these structures are great, and a lot of the big house builders buy and control their land this way. Once we gain planning, we have a time frame to complete the deal. This is a timeframe we can control through the planning process, so it allows us to find the funds required to complete the purchase as and when we are ready. We may want to finish off a site and release funds from sales, or it may be the start of winter, and we'll complete in the spring once we are ready to start on-site.

If you're buying some land or property with outline planning permission, then there will still be some things to complete in order to obtain full planning permission and get started on-site. These are known as reserved matters, which are:

- **Access** - The accessibility to and from the site in a safe manner for cars, cyclists, and pedestrians

- **Scale** - How big the properties are going to be, including ridge heights

- **Layout** - The way in which the buildings sit and are oriented within the site, taking into account existing developments

- **Materials** - The external materials used, such as bricks, roof tiles, and windows
- **Landscaping** - What landscaping will be done to enhance the development

Often, you'll be the one to sort these out with your architect as the vendors usually leave it for the developer to do their own thing, subject to planning approval. One thing we typically do is use the same roof tiles, window colour, bricks, etc, on every development to keep things simple and understand our build costs.

There may be some pre-commencement conditions to get approved and carried out before you actually get started on the build. These could be things like creating a new access, demolition, relocating a telegraph pole, etc. Some conditions are pre-habitation, such as street signs, footpaths, and lighting. These conditions can be quick or often painfully slow to release. We've been waiting for a pre-commencement condition to be released for over a year now. It's crazy, but the planners are overstretched, and in our case, it's not holding things up because we have a pipeline of developments at different stages, but don't let these catch you out waiting to get started.

Planning is typically granted for three years, but some councils are now only giving two years. This is to encourage vendors not to sit on land with planning for a long time and get more houses built. As long as you make a start on certain things within this time frame, you can retain the planning.

A planning notice is usually put up outside the plot once planning has been submitted and validated. This is to notify the public of the application and give them the chance to have their say. These notices are put up on nearby telegraph poles if there is nowhere to pin the notice. I live in a windy part of the country called the Fens, so the notices outside our plots tend to blow away the minute they are put up, and we don't really get many objections. They don't make drawing pins like they used to, you know?!

Often, there can be many objections from neighbours and even from people who don't even live anywhere near the site. The councils then read through the list of objections and take them into account when giving you permission or refusal; they do have to be valid points though, rather than people's personal opinions. A lot of people object because they don't like change or disruption, which is only temporary, and some even due to plain old jealousy. You do see some classic objections, such as:

- A woman complained because she would be able to see the proposed house while she stood in her bath.

- A neighbour saying that the light from a window would spoil the view of the moon through her daughter's telescope.

- Over his dead body will a house be built as it would block out his view. He died, and planning was approved.

- The house would block my phone signal, and the front door faces the street.

- It will be too noisy while it's being built, and the builders will be able to see into our garden.

- No one will buy them, and they will all be rented out to single moms.

- Neighbours objecting to a new build because it would ruin their shortcut to the beach.

- There's not enough parking in the street; someone could have a birthday party, and there will be cars parked everywhere.

- A neighbour saying the paint from the new house would come off in strips and start flapping in the wind, keeping them awake.

- I used to have the nicest house on the street, and now I won't, so stop it.

- A neighbour objected to a new house being built because they may have a barbecue, and it would be offensive because they were vegan.

If planning does get refused, then you can resubmit. Upon refusal, you'll be able to see the issues that need addressing. Some of these might be simple amendments, while others might seem ludicrous. This gives you the chance to appeal if you think there's a solid case. You get 3 minutes to fight your corner, and if this is something you feel would be better done by your architect or planning consultant, then let them do it before you start ranting about how useless they all are and get thrown out. Many appeals are won at committee meetings, so don't let refusal be the end of the road to build out your developments and provide the much-needed homes.

Don't be put off by planning; it's just a process to go through, and if you have a good architect and planning consultant, you'll be able to breeze through successfully in most instances.

Summary

1. Planning can be a complicated process that you chip away at one piece at a time. Starting with outline planning skips some of the early stages, meaning you can get started on-site sooner.

2. Outline planning gives you certainty of the number of units. This de-risks you from the very outset.

3. Using a planning consultant on sensitive schemes can help

you more likely get the planning permission than just using an architect because they fully understand the planning policy.

4. Don't be afraid to change an existing planning scheme to a better one. Sometimes the deals just don't stack, or the house types may not suit your target market.

5. More houses doesn't mean more profit. Look at reducing the units by building larger houses rather than more smaller ones to reduce build costs and increase your profits.

6. Appeals don't mean it's the end of the road for the application. See if the issues can be resolved, resubmit a better scheme, and get the committee on your side.

7. Use a planning consultant to speak on your behalf at an appeal; they know what to say and, more importantly, what not to say to the committee.

8. Expect some objections from neighbours as they don't like change. The objections have to be valid objections and not personal objections, so most will be ignored instantly.

9. Access is the most important reserved matter to release out of the five. You can use reserved matters to control the planning application to your advantage.

10. Check if the area you are looking to develop in has CIL payable, as this can often make the smaller deals less viable.

CHAPTER SIX

Appraising the Sites

"No matter how many mistakes you make or how slow you progress, you are still way ahead of everyone who isn't trying" - **Tony Robbins.**

Understanding the build costs is one of the areas I see so many people struggle with while possibly being the most important out of all of the 8 steps. Underprice your build costs and you could pay too much for the land and run out of money through the build, and you definitely don't want that. Overpricing the build costs and you'll be walking away from developments that could have been perfect for you to get that life-changing 6 or 7-figure profit.

In order to see if the land we are looking at is a viable deal, we need to understand all the costs associated from the start to the end. There are professional fees, surveys, legals, finance, planning, and not to forget what it's actually going to cost to build the site out. I use a deal analyser that I've created in which I enter all of these costs, and it soon tells me if it's a deal or no deal. It even tells me what the maximum price is that we can actually pay for the site. This saves me a lot of time, and it roughly takes me around 15 minutes to appraise a site with this deal analyser.

One of the first things we need to do is establish the gross development value (GDV). This would be the value of the house you are looking to build, or if you were to build more houses and different types such as 2-bed bungalows and 3-bed houses, then the total of all these combined. The valuations you can get can vary significantly, but you need to be accurate with this figure because you work your way backwards from GDV to find the true land value.

Next are the build costs, and as mentioned earlier, we need to add many things together to work this out. Some of these will be assumptions and some can be accurate costs. Build costs are broken down into 2 elements. First, you have hard costs such as the house structure, foundations, utilities, externals, demolition/site clearance, and preliminaries.

The house structure is everything from damp-proof course upwards (DPC) and includes kitchens, bathrooms, stairs, etc; everything to fully finish the property inside known as turnkey. You may hear people talking about their build costs, and they are usually based on a cost per square meter or per square foot; we usually use the latter. You need to know this cost at the appraisal stage because usually, you don't have all the details and therefore need to work out how much the house is going to cost depending on how big it is. Plus, the last thing you want to do is spend a load of money getting something accurately costed to the penny that you might not even buy. Most of the time, you won't even have enough information to get a site costed up, especially if you are just looking at a piece of land with no planning.

With the foundations, there are lots of different types to suit different ground conditions, the structure, the existing trees, or the trees that are being removed that we talked about earlier in the book. These foundation costs can vary as much as 100%, and in some cases, more. There may be some sites that are restricted by room available so you have to choose a certain type such as driven piles that may push up the costs.

Stronger foundations seem to be specified more frequently these days from structural engineers to protect themselves from being sued if a foundation were to fail on design. Material and labour costs have also skyrocketed in the past few years so your costs need to be current and up to date. One thing we do look at to reduce our costs is to see if we can keep the soil on site and spread it out in the gardens as we have pretty good silt soil where we live. This not only saves money but also a lot of lorries coming in and out of the site, which cuts down on the mud on the road and keeps the neighbours happy.

With every new build, you are going to have to install water, electric, drainage, and possibly gas while it's still allowed. Each house will have a separate supply, but you may be able to share the main drainage connection which will reduce the costs. We allow a certain amount of money per utility per house, and like most things, these have increased over the past few years and quite significantly. The utility companies are extremely short-staffed and are passing on rising costs to their customers like everyone else has been doing.

White diesel is just one of those costs that has been passed on to their customers recently due to a Government change. The construction industry used to be allowed to use red diesel in their plant machinery, which was half the price of white diesel, the same type you get at your usual petrol station. Now we have to pay pump prices, which are expensive, and when you get costs that double overnight, it can have a big impact on businesses' survival. A company can't simply absorb an increase like that, especially on the scale these companies use it in their big machines, so it is passed on to the next person.

We usually pay for our utilities and get them booked in, but there have been times when the utility companies ask for more money which by then you don't have much choice but to pay. This is often the case if you choose third-party companies or their 90-day quote has expired by the time you get on site and require them. They also get it wrong from time to time, just expect the unexpected and it will be fine. Utility companies have to be booked well in advance, and even when they give you a date, they will prioritise emergency works over yours.

Unfortunately, none of the companies will work in the same trench together or use the traffic management system. So, the utility companies will be back and forth, digging up the road, connecting their utilities, backfilling, and making good the tarmac, only for another company to start digging up the road and doing the same a couple of weeks later. This again adds to the time it takes, especially if they need to apply for a permit and dig out the same hole a week later. Residents really get fed up with this, which is understandable.

On a recent site, we had Anglian Water connecting our plots to the water main. It was shown on the drawings to be 1 m in the road away from the curbs. As they started digging, they found another main pipe that was closer to the curb. They thought this was the water main, so they drilled into it, only to find out it was an old gas main which smelled really bad. Luckily, it wasn't a live one, but this did cause a few days' delay, which can mean no deliveries in and out of the site.

Externals need to be factored into your build deal analyser. This includes the outside area around the property, such as roads, driveways, gardens, fencing, etc. Unlike the big house builders who provide six paving slabs, we do install a decent-sized patio. Yes, they cost more money, but we know they make a huge difference to sales because the buyers don't need to spend money to make it bigger once they've moved in or pay a fortune to have this added on as an extra when they complete on the property. Go above and beyond your buyers' expectations, and your properties will stand out compared to the others that they view, resulting in quicker and better sales.

We often gravel our drives, which helps with the drainage. These are also cheaper and quicker to install. With the roads, we stick to tarmac. This is done by a specialist contractor and is very quick to do. You just need to make sure they are booked well in advance to your program of work, and you're definitely ready for them because sometimes they can be booked 3-4 months ahead. If there are major roadworks going on nearby, then these contracts will take priority over the batching plants. And if you miss the slot with your guys, then you could be adding an additional 3-4 months onto your site, all while your finance is racking up daily interest charges. We prefer permeable tarmac over permeable block paving as it looks and lasts a lot longer. Block paving can sink and soon discolour within a matter of months, whereas the tarmac stays looking fresh for many years to come. Tarmac is also much quicker; they can be in and out within a couple of days rather than a few weeks of block paving. The tarmac transforms a site instantly, and we have one coming up shortly, which is probably one of the nicest smells on a construction site you can get.

In some cases, you may purchase land with a building that needs to be demolished. We've bought a few like this, and often properties from the 50s and 60s came on large plots, as land was cheap and everyone had a large vegetable plot. Some of the houses we've bought to demolish have been the old prefab houses that were built after the war. These were only designed to last for 10 years, but people still live in them today. The pre-fabs are usually full of asbestos and not very well insulated, which makes them not mortgageable, limiting the number of buyers who can purchase them as they'll have to do this with cash only.

You do need permission to demolish the property, and there will be conditions stipulated. Most of these would be from a safety point of view, such as erecting fencing, dust suppression, asbestos, etc. A property will usually undergo a soft strip out before demolition, and these are done by hand. This is where any scrap copper can be removed. Often, the plastic windows and the plasterboard will be put into separate skips for recycling. This is so that when the building is taken down with a machine, it's easier to clear the materials away, as there will just be timber and rubble left. Timber may be skipped, or in our town, we are allowed to burn it on-site. Rubble can be crushed and reused on-site where possible, which may reduce your demolition costs. A house can typically be demolished and cleared in just one day once the soft strip out is done.

To protect and run your site consists of preliminaries. These are the things required to get the job done, but many don't factor in the costs, which can soon add up. First, you need to secure the site with fencing. We usually use metal Heras-style fencing, which we buy off eBay. If you need top security and want to keep nosey people out, then timber 8ft hoarding is best, but certainly more expensive. You'll need site cabins for workers, toilets, and secure storage. Temporary power and water are required until the properties are connected. Any plant hire, such as diggers, dumpers, telehandlers, etc., is also necessary.

I often get asked why we don't buy our own plant, and there are some simple reasons that align with our business plan. Machines are expensive to buy, so it can mean laying out lots of cash or committing to running and maintenance overheads. We use quite a few different size diggers for different tasks, so we would need 3-5 machines. The machines often break down quite a bit. Hydraulic hoses regularly leak or blow, which are simple fixes. But with the newer machines having far more electronics, we are seeing a lot of electrical issues that cause the machine to go into limp mode or shut down until the manufacturers can come out and reboot it.

Sometimes we have 3 or 4 diggers and 2 or 3 dumpers onsite, and other times we have 1 of each. As we work through the summers and not the winters, the plant would sit around doing nothing, and machines are better being used daily than every now and again, as things will perish. We would also have to pay to have the plant moved on and offsite every time and pay for a yard to store it in. The insurance isn't cheap either, as they are high theft items. There are lots more reasons, but it makes sense for us to hire in the latest plant as and when we need it, with minimal hassle, and just factor this into our costs. As my sons figure out what direction they want to go long term, either continuing to be seasonal developers or scaling up and doing larger sites, this may change, and they start to buy their own machines. Whatever they choose, I'll support them all the way. Simply put, plant machinery has a cost whether you own it or hire it in, and needs to be factored into your appraisal.

Will you have a site agent or do this yourself? As much as I have over 35 years of construction knowledge, things change. When my sons quit their apprenticeships to become full-time developers, we all enrolled in an SMSTS course so we could set up and run our sites safely. This is a 5-day course and the highest level of safety construction qualification. I remember the first day when the instructor asked if just the two of us could go outside, as he wanted to discuss something in private. He said he didn't think it was a good idea bringing my 18-year-old sons here, as they will fail the exam, and that most people who come to take their SMSTS are in their 40s or 50s and have years of site experience and are already in a foreman-type role. I said no problem, I'm sure they will learn something. After the 5 days of sitting there listening and writing, both my sons (and I before you ask) passed, whereas some of the other guys who had been in construction for years failed. The instructor was amazed and said my sons had participated more than the others and they were a credit to me. Unfortunately, we live in a world where people get judged on their limiting beliefs rather than giving people a chance to prove themselves first.

If you do decide to run your own projects, then you can get paid on average £4000 a month to do so. It does depend on the size of the project and your experience, and in some cases, you can get paid more. Lenders are happy to pay this as they see you will be more committed to the development full time. This cashflow can allow you to quit what you are currently doing much sooner and become a paid developer full time. If you're a tradesperson, you can pay yourself for any work you do, and then there's the big chunk of developers' profit at the back end that you'll get also. There is no other strategy out there that pays you several times on or throughout your own projects.

Something that often gets forgotten about in people's build costs is a contingency. This is your cash buffer factored in just in case there are some unforeseen circumstances, such as having to excavate the foundations deeper due to poor ground conditions. This cash buffer can be used, and you still make your predicted profit. If everything goes okay, then this cash buffer contingency just gets added to your profit. For first-time developers, lenders will want to see an 8-10% contingency on your build costs. If your project was going to cost £500,000 to build, then an additional £50,000 would be factored in for the unforeseen.

I'll give you an example of a recent one we had on our site. We were installing the underground drainage to one of our sites, and the fittings and inspection chambers were really expensive. A good friend of mine, Frank, was helping out on our site for a day and he couldn't believe the prices I was paying. He told me a place online to buy from where it was 90% cheaper, so we switched brands halfway through. We continued with all the drainage, and one of the things we like to do before we start installing the finished groundworks is to test the drains. We do this by putting expandable bungs in the outlets, then filling the drainage system up with water. We leave this overnight, and if the water level is still there, then it's fine. If it's dropped, then we know we have a leak somewhere. This can sometimes be from one of the rubber seals getting pinched when putting them together or missing.

The day we were about to fill up and test the drains was after a night of heavy rain, and upon lifting the inspection chamber lids, we could see water rushing in around the rings and the blanking plugs. This was from the water pressure in the ground going into the pea gravel, which surrounds the pipe, then finding its way through the fittings. None of us had seen anything like this before, and the only way to fix this was to dig around the chambers and seal them. I know what you're thinking here, in that the leaks were coming from the materials that were 90% cheaper, and I always say, "buy cheap, you pay twice." But it was the expensive items I bought from the builders' merchants that were faulty; the cheaper items worked perfectly. Others who bought the faulty stuff would have the same issues, but many don't do the testing if they are working round customers' houses, so they wouldn't know about the faults. I did have a couple of people comment on my posts on Instagram, so it wasn't just us. In this case, it was quicker to pay my groundworkers to rectify the problem than take everything back, so this did come at an additional cost, which just comes out of the contingency and does not affect the predicted profit.

Another instance, I told my sons to insulate the loft and get everything done up there as soon as it's boarded and not after it's plastered, in case they put their foot through the ceiling. They got distracted on other jobs while I was away running a business planning retreat in Cyprus, and one of them slipped and put their foot through the ceiling. Being twins, the other son did exactly the same the week after, so I had to pay for the plasterer to redo 2 ceilings. Good thing we have a contingency. This is how some people, including myself, learn by making mistakes, so maybe my sons will do the insulation before the plasterers skim next time. We shall see.

If a project overruns from delays with materials, bad weather, or bad project management, then finance costs will increase. Materials can get stolen not just from break-ins but sometimes from the trades who work on-site. We also get damage done by other trades on-site who are careless in the way they work. Scratches on kitchen units, chips in worktops, and just general breakages all need to be paid for, and the contingency is there for this unless a trade owns up and foots the bill. Pigs flying comes to mind right now.

The second set of costs are soft costs, which consist of Architect fees, legal fees, surveys, finance, etc.

You will be working with lots of professionals from start to finish, and we refer to these people as our power team. They have the experience, knowledge, and contacts to make your developments happen. These might not be cheap, but in most cases, you get what you pay for. These are some of the essential members of your power team that you need:

Solicitors: You'll need 2 types, a conveyancing solicitor to deal with the sale of the properties, and a solicitor for the land purchase. This needs to be a commercial solicitor who can work on what can sometimes be complex purchases where several landowners or titles are involved. Buying land is different from land that has already been built on because there are lots more things to check, which leads to greater costs, whereas a house that's already built has had this done, maybe several times over.

I've worked with many solicitors, and what I will say is, there are solicitors, and there are solicitors. It's taken me years of trial and error to find the perfect power team that knows what they are actually doing. Many solicitors have tried to charge me stamp duty wrongly on land and property purchases, and when I've challenged this, after some pushback from the solicitors, they usually come back to me and admit I was right. This has saved me and my mentees thousands of pounds of money that they said was wrongly due to HMRC. The silence you get on the other end of the phone when you ask the solicitor the question "How many years have you been doing this and how many people have paid unnecessary stamp duty based on your advice?" You can hear a pin drop, but ultimately, HMRC is not going to come knocking on your door trying to hand the money back that you shouldn't have paid in the first place, so it's down to you and your solicitor to make sure it's done right in the first place.

Brokers - A broker is someone who seeks funding for your development from a variety of lenders. This can be 100% for the build and fees and even a contribution towards the land, reducing the equity amount you need to put in. Again, there are brokers, and there are brokers. I can genuinely say I wouldn't be where I am (or many of my mentees) if it wasn't for my broker, so make sure you get a good one because they can make a huge difference. My broker used to be a lender and understands more than most brokers because he fully understands what the lenders are looking for. He specialises in getting first-time developers their funding and looks for long-term relationships on the basis that if he provides a great service above other brokers, you will use their services again and again, and the borrowing will be larger. Some brokers won't entertain loans under £500,000 or without a proven track record because they get paid a fee based on the loan size, and first-time developers will always require more work at the beginning.

Brokers have to do a huge amount of work upfront and only get paid on completion, most often by the lender and not you directly, so you can see why a lot of brokers just want the easy pickings. Some brokers charge an initial fee of around £500, a commitment fee if you like. I'm not saying stay away from the brokers that charge the upfront fee, but make sure they don't just take your money and don't do any work for it. Many brokers work upfront for free, so they will only get paid once they have done all the work.

Architects - Architects will assist you throughout the development process, but primarily at the beginning to take a site through planning or create detailed working drawings for Building Control that the trades can use. I would advise finding an architect who has experience with similar-sized projects as the one you'll be working on. I have an architect who handles all of our sites ranging from 1 to 10 units, and a RIBA qualified architect who works on large commercial conversions, as they have completed over 20 similar-sized projects and can provide valuable expertise. Prices can vary greatly, so make sure to shop around and compare quotes that are comparable, rather than simply looking for the cheapest option. A good architect will design a scheme from the developer's perspective, keeping the designs and materials simple. One thing to check is whether your architect has the capacity to complete your plans and submit them within your timeframe, as many architects work on multiple projects at once. This could mean that your project is worked on one day a week over 5-6 weeks, rather than having one person in a larger company working on your project full-time. Architects take vacations, get sick, and have other personal commitments, so it's important to address this from day one to avoid significant delays.

Planning consultants - These professionals can help you optimise your scheme, as many architects tend to play it safe in order to obtain planning permission on the first try and avoid upsetting the planning department. Planning consultants have a deep understanding of planning policies, and some are particularly skilled at finding and using loopholes. It's often worthwhile to engage a planning consultant at the beginning of a site, rather than only calling them if your initial application is rejected. People often ask me whether they should use a local planning consultant, and there is no definitive answer. However, a local planning consultant may possess exceptional knowledge about the specific council's requirements and preferences. They may have established relationships with planners and a track record of success with other developers that can benefit your applications. On the other hand, utilising a planning consultant who operates nationally can also be advantageous, as they will have experience dealing with a wide range of councils and can bring that expertise to your area.

Mentors - A mentor is someone who's been there and done what you want to do. They handhold you through the development and can fast-track your results. Not many people have mentors, so this leaves them open to learning on the job, which can then result in slow progress or expensive mistakes. A mentor should give you access to their black book of contacts that they've taken years to put together. This will include their commercial solicitor, broker, private investors, etc. This alone is usually worth far more than their mentoring fees. A mentor can also be there if any issues arise throughout the development, to sense-check deals, advise on how to negotiate a better deal for you.

One of my mentees saved over £40,000 in stamp duty after I insisted he tell his solicitor to check it out and do it correctly. It took over 3 attempts and then finally the solicitor agreed, saving him a huge amount of money. This clearly shows that your power team save or make you money, not cost you money.

Surveys - During the purchase phase, you may have to carry out some surveys to check things or get conditions released before completing the deal. Surveys range from £400 to £1500. Here are a few common ones:

Topography - This is where the site is measured using technology to relay information to the architect and, more importantly, to make sure you are getting what you pay for. I've seen a developer buy a site for planning of 7 units, and once he was on site setting out the 7th unit, it didn't fit, meaning it would affect his profit hugely. He also had to go back to planning and resubmit a whole new scheme, which caused delays. The survey also checks land heights, neighbouring building heights, tree locations, etc.

Ground investigation survey - Can be done manually or with boring machines to see what soil makes up the ground or for contamination results purposes. The soil is checked in a laboratory. A remediation plan then needs to be put in place.

Ecology survey - To see what wildlife is currently there, what provisions need to be put in place, and what the site will be like for wildlife afterwards. You may have to put up bird boxes, replace trees that have been taken out, newt protection fences around the perimeter, bat surveys, etc. Some ecology surveys can determine which months you can or can't carry out the work. This often catches a lot of newbie developers out.

Asbestos survey - A legal requirement for demolition. Never assume there isn't any asbestos in the ground, especially on old farm sites and garden plots. People have been burying this stuff for years. I know a developer who discovered asbestos when he was excavating where the road was going in, and this cost him £100,000 to have removed, plus caused delays to his site. Even more reason to have a contingency that we mentioned earlier, but prevention is better than cure.

Arboricultural survey - A survey on the trees that may need to be removed, remain, or be replaced. If there are protected trees, then a survey may be needed, and a protection plan should be put in place.

As you can see, there are a large number of things to factor into your deal appraisal. Once you understand this, you can appraise sites quickly and accurately, moving on to the offer stage, which is the next step in the Property Developer's Blueprint.

Summary

1. It's important to know your build cost £ per square foot or £ per square meter in your goldmine area. You can then appraise sites quickly and accurately.

2. Get accurate sold prices together to ensure your GDVs are realistic and not overinflated just to make the deal work. We focus on recent sold prices, not for sale prices.

3. Look at professional fees as zero cost because in most cases, they pay for themselves or allow you to earn far greater profits from their experience and knowledge.

4. You will get quicker at appraising sites; the main thing is to get

it right first, then speed will come. The more you practice, the better you will become.

5. Material prices can fluctuate, especially in property cycles and always heading North on January 1st by around 10%. Make sure you factor in the increase when you will be buying materials, not in today's prices.

6. Decide if you want to manage your own projects and pay yourself £4000 per month or employ a project manager or use a main contractor.

7. An 8-10% contingency should be factored in for first-time developers; this will be required by lenders also and should be seen as additional profit if you don't need to dip into this throughout the build.

8. Check to see what utilities are available, and bear in mind that utility prices have risen sharply over the past few years. Make sure you factor in the correct cost.

9. Ensure you have an asbestos survey done before demolishing anything pre-year 2000; check if there are any materials that you can sell or recycle to reduce costs.

10. There are quite a few professional fees to factor in, and one that often gets missed is a mentor. A mentor can fast track your results and handhold you through developments because they've been there and done it multiple times.

CHAPTER SEVEN

Putting in your Offer

"If you don't risk anything, you risk everything" - **Rob Moore.**

Putting in offers isn't simply a case of emailing the agent a price you're hoping the vendor will take. This is what the other 99% do, and we want to separate ourselves from these people, stand out, and position ourselves so we look like we know what we are doing, especially as a newbie to property development. I always believe you only get one chance to make a first impression, so let's talk about how we can get that right.

First, we need to understand the purpose of the offer. This is to present a proposal that is fair and that the vendor will be happy with the offer as well. Too little offered, and the vendor can feel insulted, or the agent can feel embarrassed even submitting it, knowing that the vendor will want answers as to why it is so much lower from the asking price that the agent suggested they market it for.

Many agents don't even submit the low offers, even though they are legally obliged to submit every offer, which is a big reason why we need to build relationships with agents and explain our offers. I believe you should always make an offer where both parties feel like it is a win-win - you get the land for a price that works for you and you make a 25% profit, and the vendor gets to sell their land for a price they feel happy with. If the imbalance is too great, they will soon start telling their friends and family, and they will all persuade them that they've been ripped off and could have got another 20 million pounds more. Okay, so the amount might be an exaggeration, but I've seen it time and time again where you can agree to a deal with a vendor, they then start telling people, and they ruin it for both parties, leaving the vendor and the developer frustrated.

So, how do we stand out from the competition? We use what's called an offer pack. This pack consists of details about the site, planning, pros and cons, the numbers, comparable sold properties, our contact information, and more importantly, what we are prepared to offer with some substance to what that offer price is. These are in glossy A4 brochures which you can leave with the vendors and agents, or you can have them on your phone electronically. You should carry these packs everywhere you go because of the 3ft rule, telling everyone what you are doing. Just imagine if you were in a hotel, cafe, builders merchants, and you get talking to someone about what you are doing and you can whip out your offer pack right there and then. You can explain by showing them your nice, professional-looking glossy brochure or get someone's email address and send it over to them electronically. These people might want to invest in your projects, and one of my mentees has had his deal funded of £500,000 simply by telling his scaffolder and showing him the offer pack. Even if they are not immediately interested in investing, I guarantee they will be once they see you on site doing what you said you would do and they realise they've missed out on an opportunity to make money hands off.

Your offer pack allows the agent and vendor to look through your proposal, do a bit of due diligence on you, check out your social media (make sure you delete the drunken night out on the weekend images), take a look at your website, and position your company as a trusted go-to business. Being able to stand behind this as a first-time developer can really help with imposter syndrome. Compare this to a cash offer email from everyone else, and you can see why you will start to stand out and get your offers accepted. I often produce proof of funds for my mentees, so they can get their offers taken more seriously as the agent can see the cash is there rather than a false promise like the others do, which works really well.

Land is often very overpriced, as discussed earlier, this is so that agents can get their vendors onto their books and get a little commission. Half of the problem is they don't really know how to value land, and they still use an old rule of a third, a third, a third that worked about 20 years ago. This is a third for the GDV for the land, a third of the GDV for the build, and a third of GDV for the profit. If only this were true in today's world, but it isn't, and this is where you may need to educate your agent that we do still live on planet earth.

The rule of thumb these days is more like 25% for the profit, 50% for the build and fees, and 25% for the land purchase. So if a development is worth, say, £1m, then you shouldn't be paying much more than 25% of GDV as your build costs are what your build costs are; therefore, it will reduce your profit. Lenders will want to see a profit of 25% on GDV or 20% profit on total costs after finance, so unless you are your own bank, you have to stick to this criteria. If an agent has overinflated the valuation, then there could be quite a bit of work to get the vendor down to our level of thinking, but definitely not impossible. It's not often that difficult because once you demonstrate your numbers with the ideal working, then put in the agent's number, it throws the deal straight off. This builds credibility and trust with you pretty much instantly.

I agreed to a site with a vendor far below what it was worth by demonstrating my numbers to them. The vendor responded to a direct-to-vendor letter drop that I had done. She gave me a call, asked me to come round, so I took my son to the viewing. It was for a 3-bedroom detached bungalow that belonged to her father, who was suffering from early dementia. She wanted to move him nearer to where she lived in Leeds because she was concerned he might have a fall and she wouldn't know about it.

She had the bungalow valued by an estate agent for £125,000. Sounds cheap for a 3-bed bungalow in Lincolnshire, but the property had a lot of asbestos throughout. It was non-standard construction and on a cesspit drainage system, so therefore, no one could get a mortgage on it. She was looking for a quick cash sale. I asked her what the lowest price was that she was prepared to sell for, and she said £70,000. At this stage, I haven't even offered, but you can see the woman isn't that interested in getting a high price but more of a deal done right now so she can move her dad as soon as possible near to where she lives.

I explained I would run some numbers and send over an offer later by email that evening, which is exactly what I did. My starting offer was for £52,283. Had I gone in too low and blown it? Early the next morning, I received an email saying that if I could increase my offer to £55,000 so that it covers her solicitor's fee, then we have a deal to which I agreed. The next day, she went back to Leeds and took her father with her.

A lot of people don't believe that you can get deals like this, but I've done a few at around 50% below the open market value. They simply don't know how to do them, but instead of learning, they will keep that fixed mindset, which does not serve people very well. It really comes down to the vendors' motivation and how quickly they want to move on. We went on to gain planning for a large 5-bed house and sold it for a £190,000 profit. This is a prime example of a win-win, whereby the seller gets what they want (to sell fast for cash) and we get what we want (a development with at least £100,000 profit).

Once you've got your offer packs done, you need to put the offer forward. In most cases, the first offer will be refused, even if the vendor is motivated to sell. So never let this be your best offer. We find that a 2nd offer has a better chance of getting accepted, and even more so on the third offer, as this is where you make it seem like you can't offer anymore.

I actually love the negotiation stage, as this is one of my strengths and where I help my mentees a lot, especially when they are going back and forth with the vendors. Finding out why the vendor is selling is one of the first things you should be asking, as some will just want to get rid of it, whereas other vendors are still emotionally attached to their gardens and may want a higher price. Once you understand this, you get to know whether they want certainty, speed, or price. If it's certainty they want, they might be prepared to hold out for a higher price. If it's speed because they need the money for something, then they will often be prepared to sell at a discount.

Some vendors may be interested in doing a joint venture with you. These types of structures allow you to pay the highest price, and you may be wondering why you would want to pay a higher price. If it means putting no money in for the purchase and still making an amazing profit, then it means you can do as many of these as you want. The benefits of working with vendors are huge, but you also have to remember that when the vendor gets paid their slice out of the deal, they may become one of your investors in your next deal because you've built up a good relationship and trust over the previous months.

We usually put 2 offers forward in our packs. This may be a cash offer, a JV offer, or an option, for example. If you give the vendors only 1 offer, then it is most likely going to be a yes or no. Provide them with 2 offers, and they will steer towards one more than the other because one will naturally seem more attractive. You can also make the offer you would like them to choose look more attractive than the other one.

Once you get lots of offers out, you will realise that it is a numbers game. For every 20 offers, you may get 1-2 deals accepted. Get 100 offers out and you get 8-10 deals accepted. The more you do, the more chances you have of getting offers accepted. If the answer from the vendor is no, then you're no worse off than before. We've discussed earlier in the book that if you can meet the vendor, you will have a 90% greater chance of getting a deal accepted. This is because they will have met you hopefully on more than one occasion, and you have built up enough trust. When you show them your nice offer pack with a detailed explanation of how you have arrived at your offer, they will be more likely to accept your proposal.

If we are dealing directly with a vendor, then we like to sit down face to face and run through our offers, and take plenty of time to answer any questions they have while we are there. We'll often leave the offer pack with them and say we'll follow up in a few days, giving them time to look at the proposal. At no point do we want to pressure them, as this is a big thing for vendors and probably quite daunting if they've not sold anything in the past 30, 40, or 50+ years where the sales process is mostly electronic now.

Ultimately, we want to give the vendor an offer that they will be very happy with, a service where we go above and beyond, and one where we handhold them through the whole process, even supplying them with a solicitor if they don't already have one. This way, they don't take no notice from jealous friends and family members who don't want them to sell the land and make a load of tax-free money or sell on the kids' inheritance. Honestly, money does strange things to some vendors' family and friends, and I've heard all sorts of things from the many purchases we've made over time.

We very rarely have a vendor pull out of the deal due to external influences, although we did have one vendor who agreed to sell their land and was very happy with the price that we proposed. We were also going to pay them interest on their funds they were lending into the deal, and then at the last minute, their accountant of many years told them it was too risky, and the deal couldn't be done this way. The vendor was gutted that his accountant put a stop to it when he really wanted to do it. I questioned myself on whether the accountant had actually taken the money out of the business himself and didn't want the vendor to find out. Trust me, it happens to a lot of people who are too busy and have plenty of money. Their agents and accountants take the money, and they don't even notice. Some you win, and some you lose. This can get frustrating at the start of your journey, but over time, these just become pipeline deals. If they come off, they do, and if they don't, there will always be another one coming by next week.

If your offers don't get accepted, or you get outbid, then don't despair - it's all part of the process. A high percentage of deals fall through because people offer too much in the first place. Then the valuation down values the deal, meaning a lot more equity has to be put in, or the lenders won't lend. I see lots of people overestimate the numbers just to convince themselves it's a great deal and to make the deal look sexy, but you have to stick to the rules where the GDV, build costs, and profit need to be accurate.

Often, you will see many of these deals coming back to you around 3, 6, or 9 months later. A good number of people I mentor succeed in winning these deals later on, rather than at the beginning of their journey. It really comes down to getting plenty of offers out and being patient for one to be accepted. I do have many people from my Property Developers Academy who get deals accepted within their first month, but I would say more get deals accepted within that 6 and 9-month period that they offered on in their first month of starting.

A large percentage of these deals get accepted at a lower price than they originally offered because, by now, the vendor is super motivated. The target you should be aiming for is to get a deal accepted within the first 90 days, then another deal every 90-180 days after this, so you create a pipeline. Once you get your first deal, you can afford to negotiate a little harder or wait for a more motivated vendor to accept a lower offer.

Summary

1. Offer packs work and make you stand out much better from the competition who just email in a number.

2. Expect the first offer to be refused, so never make this your highest offer. The third offer has the highest chance of acceptance.

3. Submitting 2 offers gives the vendor a choice, and they will steer towards one over the other, so make the one you want them to choose more attractive.

4. Putting in offers is a numbers game - the more deals you offer on, the more chances you have of offers being accepted. Your target should be 1 in 20.

5. Deals have a habit of coming back on the market 3, 6, and 9 months later after the vendors get messed about by timewasters. This is why you build good relationships with vendors and agents so that they come back to you first.

6. Carry your glossy offer packs everywhere you go and have an electronic version on your phone so you can tell everyone what you do. You could get more land or investors wanting to put funds into your deals after they've seen an offer pack.

7. Doing joint ventures with landowners can be a great way to not have to put equity into a deal. This means there is no limit on how many deals you can do.

8. When you pay a vendor for the land, they may want to become one of your investors once they've seen you build the site out and

got to know you better. Sow the seed early on.9. Make sure your agent always puts your offer in; if they don't, then find the vendor and send it yourself. This will make the agent look like they can't be trusted.

9. Explain the 25/50/25 rule to the agents and tell them that the 33/33/33 rule doesn't work anymore due to high building and labour costs. The sooner you do this, the better, so they don't disregard any low offers that you submit.

CHAPTER EIGHT

Funding your Development

"Take all the training you can get, just one idea is all you need to save yourself from years of hard work" - **Brian Tracey.**

Finding the money to purchase and build out your site is the step that is probably going to be the one that people think they will struggle with, so let's get one thing clear: there is more money in the world right now than ever before. Yes, you read that right, and we know this because the governments around the world have been printing it in their trillions. Money doesn't just disappear either, it flows around the planet at lightning speed from those who understand how to collect money to those that understand how to spend it, and trust me, there is definitely no shortage of these people, which is why most are skint.

Governments around the world create problems such as wars and pandemics to print money that gets distributed to the spenders, which, in turn, then changes hands to the collectors. This causes inflation, which erodes debt, and from my knowledge, there is only one country in the world debt-free, and that's Macao SAR. This is very different from the $32.9 trillion the USA currently owes, and in 2nd place, the UK with a debt of $8.7 trillion. So you can see why inflation is good for them, but it's never going to repay the debt that just keeps accumulating year after year.

It's becoming very clear from evidence that the rich and poor gap divide is also at its greatest, and there are many reasons for this, such as higher cost of living (the producers will collect money), low wages, an increase in house prices (landlords and developers reap the rewards), it's expensive to go to university, money mindset that it is scarce, having to physically work hard, feeling like a victim to the system, taxation on the masses (average class, which now drags them down lower).

Some people might not believe this, but being wealthy or poor is actually a choice, and I believe this comes down to if you accept that there is an abundance of money everywhere and that you take the right actions to become wealthy, for which there are many proven strategies to demonstrate how. There are more millionaires and billionaires on the planet than ever before, and they all leave clues as to how they make their money. For me, it's property development and leverage, not bricklaying and trading time for money like it used to be.

So now we know there is plenty of money around, and that we need a positive attitude that we will raise the necessary money when required. How do you get started in funding your developments?

Let's look at a typical development structure that I've used many times. Let's say the GDV is £400,000 with a £100,000 purchase price, a £200,000 build cost, and a £100,000 profit for you.

The lender contributes 50% towards the purchase (£50,000), and you will put in the remaining 50% (£50,000), which is known as the equity. The lender also agrees to give you 100% of the money required for the build, which is known as the senior debt (£200,000), and this is paid at certain stages as you build, known as the drawdowns. This means that for your £50,000 (or someone else's), you can make a 200% return on your money and get all of it back once you sell. You put in £50,000 and make a £100,000 profit, 200%. With tax-efficient structures, you could pay zero tax on this amount, meaning you get to keep every single penny. The bigger the deal, the bigger the numbers. This is a basic example of how developments are financed, and there would be some fees such as legal, planning, interest, etc, which are all factored into the deal.

A lender typically lends 60-65% of GDV or up to 90% of total costs and will require a 1st charge on the land as they are the senior lender who is putting in the most money and therefore taking on most of the risk. This is done by solicitors and land registry. This then gets removed once the development is sold, and the loan paid back with interest in full.

There are many lenders out there in the market who specifically understand developments and focus solely on this strategy. There are different layers of funding on top of the senior lending that can reduce your equity right down to just 2% of all money required. That means on a £1,000,000 land purchase and costs to build, you could be putting in as little as £20,000. That's why development finance can be incredible; it's a huge leverage of other people's money.

Development finance is not always the cheapest form of money, but ask yourself, could you do a development without it? If they put in most of the money and it allows you to make an amazing profit after you've paid everything off, then I'm sure the answer is yes. I've used development finance many times, made a lot of money, and built really great relationships with the lenders, whereby I can simply call them, and they will lend me what I need. My mentees usually take this route through my broker as this gets them started sooner.

You may be asking where you are going to find £50,000, but if you really want to change your life through this strategy, you will find a way. In my online and live training courses, we show 35+ ways to raise equity, and in this chapter, we'll cover a few of them.

The first place to look is family and friends, as these people will most likely have known you the longest and trust you the most. I would advise you to proceed with caution, though, as this may not be suitable for everyone due to the negativity or limiting beliefs of your family and friends. In fact, many of my mentees prefer to keep what they are doing under cover because they don't want negative comments from their nearest and dearest. In their case, and mine as well, I preferred to show people the results of what I was doing rather than tell them what I was intending to do. I knew that if I told too many people what I was about to do, they would say "You can't do that" or *"You won't do that"* or *"That's risky"*, whereas now they've seen me do it many times, they usually ask how I did it.

I have borrowed money on multiple occasions, and I only borrow this money on the condition that I will pay them interest on the loan and that I will never pay it back later than the agreed date. This keeps things simple, and when I pay this money back with the interest, they usually tell me to put it back into another development straight away because we pay far more than any bank does. In some cases, we pay 10 - 15 times more than what the banks pay. You can clearly see just how attractive it is to them to earn such a huge amount of interest, and it's a win-win situation.

I've also sold things to raise money, such as my beloved 6-berth motorhome. I thought, "Well, I'm going to be busy working, so I'm not going to be using it much, and when I make big money, I can soon buy another one that's newer and better." Don't get attached to stuff; have a look around and see what you can sell. Empty the garage and have a car boot sale, get rid of the spare car you don't use, get rid of that motorbike or jet-ski you never use, sell some of the 10 TVs you have in your house, have a good declutter, and see how much money you can gather in a short space of time. You'll be amazed. You can also start cutting back and saving money so you can pay for fees and surveys along the way. Do whatever it takes to make the first deal happen. I was already doing this, but Neville Wright, who sold Kiddycare for £70m to Morrisons, said, "You have to be prepared to go backwards to move forwards," and I totally agree with him. The problem is that too many people are stuck in their own way and not prepared to make sacrifices, even though most are just temporary. People care more about keeping up with their expensive statuses than doing what they really want to do.

Networking events can be a great way to find money for your developments. There are two main types to look at: property and business. Property networking events are great, but usually, there are more people looking for money than offering it.

This is a place where you can stand out among the crowd by speaking to everyone instead of standing in the corner on your phone. If you get the chance to introduce yourself, make sure you have what we call an elevator pitch ready. It's a 30-second intro all about you if someone were to ask you while going up or down in a lift. You should say your name and/ or company name, what you do, where you are from, and what you are looking for (private investment). This would usually have people come up to you during networking breaks if they are interested.

They may have been checking your social media while the main speaker was on (another reminder from me for you to delete those drunken night out pics). I would advise you to pick 1 or 2 networking events that you go to regularly so that you get to become known by everyone. Then, once a month, you try different networking events further afield. My wife and I have been to networking events in Scotland and even flown over to Dubai where we all know there's plenty of money. Expats who work or are retired there also want to get their money working for them, and you can help them with this.

I'm about to go to Dubai with my family. People on my social media who live there will reach out to me, so I'll go meet up and get to know them and see if we can do some business together. I always have mentees looking for funding for their deals, so I often make introductions with the people

I meet. One of my mentees has just exchanged on a development today as I write this, and I've now brought in 3 investors for them through my connections.

Business networking events seem to be better, and I'd say this is due to everyone having a business that keeps them too busy to get into property. Over recent years, businesses have been making some very good money that just sits there in their business accounts eroding away, which could be put to much better use. Lots of professionals such as solicitors, dentists, accountants all go to business networking events, and these people are what we call cash rich but time poor. One of the biggest pieces of advice I can give you about going to networking events (and in life really) is to never judge a book by its cover. I've noticed that the poorer some people look, the more money they have, and vice versa. Now I'm not saying this is always the case as some people simply ooze money externally by what they wear and how they talk. I'm just saying approach everyone as if they have money, and you won't be walking away from the investor of a lifetime.

Social media, love it or hate it, but my mentor said it can be a way to get everything you ever wanted in life, and over time, I have to agree. I wasn't on social media for years as my understanding of it was that a couple went out on a date night, didn't speak to each other throughout the date, took photos of the food before they tucked in, then posted it on Facebook so that all their friends and family (who they don't really like) would get food envy. Then they'd head off home saying how great the evening was, even though they didn't speak to each other or have eye contact. Not even a picture of the romantic couple. What's that about?

Anyway, I eventually succumbed to getting on the social media platforms, better late than never, and over time, I've gradually built up an amazing loyal audience who likes to follow our developments. Many of the loyal following have seen me go from being that 100+ hour a week bricklayer/

builder to building multiple developments, from having my ex-business partners take everything from me in 2019 to picking up my bright green Lamborghini, and a Hellcat just in case I'm in a hurry and need to look at a deal fast.

They've seen the social proof of my success, the results from the people I train and mentor, the money I raise for charity every year, the months I spend abroad with my family, and over time, this has built a lot of trust which has led me to become the UK's number one go-to person for property development training and mentoring. People will watch you over a period of time, and I know I could post on my socials asking for £1m, and this would be pledged within 48 hours from the network I've built over the past few years. This is something you should be working at on a daily or weekly basis and never stop.

Take a look at your social media. Are you only on 1 platform? Do you only have 10 followers? Do you even have a profile picture? You should be on all of them because the 1 you are on could get shut down at any point, and that may be your only source of work or way of connecting with people. There are different demographics on different platforms. LinkedIn is more business-to-business, but remember, businesses have money in their accounts, and they may have a business that is sitting on land worth far more than the business itself that they might want to sell or joint venture on.

Facebook has been around for 20 years now, and the people who were on there at the very beginning in their 30s and 40s are now in their 50s and 60s, getting inheritance, early retirement, maybe have unencumbered houses, etc. So now they have money whereas back at the beginning, they didn't.

Instagram caters to a younger audience. Most of my followers are individuals in their 30s who take pride in their work, and many tradespeople earn a good income. A mentee of mine recently secured a £500,000 investment for his project simply by talking to his scaffolder. Many tradespeople on my social media platforms come to work as subcontractors on my sites, which has been a great opportunity to get to know them.

When it comes to raising funds from private investors, it is common to use a loan agreement. It is crucial for everyone involved to understand this process, as it is the simplest way to handle the paperwork without involving the Financial Conduct Authority (FCA). It is important to note that pitching investments is only allowed when talking to qualified investors. This rule is outlined by the FCA in FCA13/3, which restricts the retail distribution of unregulated collective investment schemes and similar alternatives. If you are a detail-oriented person, this document is worth reading before bedtime.

Although not typically associated with social media, a YouTube channel offers unique advantages due to its long-lasting nature. By watching your videos, people can develop a sense of familiarity with you even before meeting in person. On the other hand, content on Facebook and Instagram feeds disappears quite quickly. Furthermore, YouTube is the second-largest search engine and is owned by Google, meaning that your videos have the potential to appear in people's searches. Through our Developing Homes YouTube channel (Please subscribe and hit the notification bell to support us), we have received various opportunities, including investment offers, land propositions, tradespeople offering their services, and individuals seeking training and mentoring after watching case studies of our mentees. Therefore, starting a YouTube channel is highly worthwhile. It demands time and effort, and you may find yourself wishing you had started years ago.

Begin by posting content whenever you go on site visits, attend networking events, or participate in investor meetings. Do not worry about perfection at the beginning, as your reach will be limited, and no one will mind. With time, you will improve, and your follower count will steadily increase. As with most things, the more effort you put into something, the more you will gain. So, start right away—today.

At the beginning, you have to get resourceful and raise the necessary funds or structure the deals creatively by using no money. This is combined with senior debt, but as you start making your profits, you can reinvest them, meaning you then have the equity part. This means you don't have to find investors or pay high interest. As you do more deals, you will start to make enough money to get to the point where you might fully fund a whole development. This does tie up your cash, but there are big savings in interest payments, arrangement fees, etc. Or you can do bigger deals as your pot of cash grows and combine this with the senior debt. I personally like to fund everything ourselves; now we are in the position we are in. Also, I'm now looking to invest in some of my mentees' developments to help them get started on their first development.

Funding used to be my biggest challenge when it came to getting into developments. I used to think you needed millions of pounds to be able to do a development, but as soon as I learned how it all works and that there are plenty of options on how to structure things, I can honestly say I've never looked back. As a result of not knowing how to, it has cost me millions of pounds in missed opportunities because you don't know what you don't know. Don't let this be you; find a good deal, and the money will come.

Summary

1. Money is in abundance. There is no shortage of money; there

is more money in the world now than ever because governments keep printing it.

2. Building your social media will build trust with your audience. Make sure you are on all the platforms demonstrating what you do.

3. People will watch you over a period of time; so make sure you post regularly about what you do, what you want to do, and what you are looking for.

4. You would be looking to put in roughly about 50% of the purchase price of the land, and the lender puts in the rest. The lender then puts in 100% of the build money and fees.

5. If you have to raise £100,000, remember this doesn't have to come from just one person. It could be made up of £40,000, £20,000, 3 x £10,000, and 2 x £5,000 from 7 sources.

6. The senior lender will always require a first charge on the land as they put in the most money and take the biggest risk.

7. Friends and family are a good place to start raising equity as they know, like, and trust you the most.

8. Find a good deal, and the money will come. It's easier to talk about borrowing money when you have a deal you are going to offer or have accepted. Offer packs work great to show people this.

9. Use loan agreements and avoid pitching your deal as an investment so you don't fall foul of FCA rules.

10. Going networking can be great for meeting potential investors. Business events work really well as there are many professionals there. Remember that you never know who you are talking to, so never judge a book by its cover.

CHAPTER NINE

Build Systems

"Do what is easy and your life will be hard, do what is hard and your life will become easy" - **Les Brown.**

The world is changing at a rapid pace. What we do today didn't work yesterday and won't work as well tomorrow, so we need to make sure that we understand what is ahead of us so we can plan for the future today.

The construction industry has always had its challenges, with a lack of skilled labour, the weather, property cycles, government policy, health and safety, and so on. One of the biggest challenges the industry faces is happening right here and now. The problem is, the UK cannot build houses fast enough to keep up with the demand. There are a number of different options that we'll be discussing in this section that may make things easier, but in reality, they all have pros and cons, and one size certainly doesn't fit all, which is why this is important to look at.

Different build systems have really evolved to the point where we can build a turnkey house on-site in just one day, yes, just one day. The challenge is that we are the UK, and we don't like change, so why are we not building this way? As with most things in the UK, we are usually very late to the party. In fact, we don't even get an invite. But on a serious note, America, Europe, Australia, and Canada are usually way ahead of the UK when it comes to changing the way they do things. Now, there's nothing wrong with letting other countries be the innovators, make some mistakes, and we copy once the system is proven to work. That's actually a sensible decision. But standing back and doing nothing about it, especially when these innovations are actual solutions to fix problems, is not.

The most common way the UK builds houses and has done for many years is to use manual labour and materials on-site following the build system, whereby the trades work in an organised sequence to deliver a predictable result. This system does work well, albeit fairly slow, with a typical house taking around 26 weeks to build, and that's only if it all goes to plan.

Why does it take so long to build a house? Well, we are using human beings after all, and they get sick, get injured, get sacked, go on holiday, wear their bodies out, and then when they turn up, it's usually too hot, too cold, too windy, too muddy, too dusty, or too wet to work. Trades are being paid very good rates of pay because there is a lack of them. My sons recognise this, which is why they wanted to get into this industry and become multi-skilled. They know that they will always be very well paid because the UK will never fill this labour shortage as they don't encourage apprenticeships anymore. Even if they did encourage apprenticeships, do you think the government gives people and businesses the confidence to take on apprentices for the next 3 years with the way they change the economy every 2 minutes? No, me neither, unfortunately. Just look at how well thatched roofers get paid because they are as rare as hen's teeth. You will be waiting months or even years for their next availability. They can also demand as much money as they want because you, the consumer, don't have much choice to go elsewhere.

Even if everything was perfect on site, why would you build a house in a field anyway? They don't build cars in a field because they want quality control and a predictable outcome. Housing is heading the same way by building more off-site now than ever.

The traditional build method of brick and block with an insulated cavity is the most common here in the UK. It's trusted by home mortgage lenders, and more importantly, with home buyers.

There's no point building something the market doesn't trust, and we're currently seeing this with electric cars. There is a lot of debate on the materials used in making the cars in comparison to their eco benefits of not using fossil fuels. Then there's the range anxiety you get from the limited power in the batteries while trying to drive to a destination, wondering if you'll make it or not. Then you have to spend time looking for somewhere to park for a long time while it charges at a higher price than petrol.

Even the garages are refusing to take EV cars in as part exchange because the batteries are £20,000+, and no warranty will cover this much, so with this and many other things, the market for EV cars isn't looking great. We've been building houses traditionally for a long time with proof that it works, the electric cars being mass-produced and the charging infrastructure hasn't, and therefore the trust isn't there.

So with the traditional way of building proven over time, why change? As I mentioned earlier, this way of construction cannot keep up with demand, and the UK is now producing poorly constructed houses due to a lack of skilled labour. So let's look at some of the alternative options available to us as developers and why we should consider using them.

Penalised systems have been around for years, and we use a lot of these construction types on our own sites today. The precision-made panels we use are timber-framed and made offsite in a factory. They are then brought to the site using a large lorry and erected on the site using a crane and a few carpenters. The frame, joists, and roof trusses are usually constructed within just 1-3 days. The benefits to us as a developer using timber frame are:

- We can be building the foundations on-site while the frame is made in the factory.

- Fixed-price contract package.

- Precision build.

- Other trades not making mistakes setting out windows, doors, and walls.

- We can build a house 4 weeks quicker than traditional build.

- It's a big chunk of the work done for us by another contractor.

- Trades can work inside the house while the bricklayers work outside.

- Work continues internally even if it's raining or snowing.

- Interest savings on development loans, meaning greater profits.

- We can sell the houses sooner, then reinvest our profits quicker.

There are many more benefits, but you can see this makes our job as developers a lot easier and much more profitable. If you look at our website www.developinghomes.co.uk, you will see just how fast some of our sites have taken us using timber frame construction.

Some of the panelised systems are now really advanced and come with windows, insulation, and even plasterboard fixed, meaning fewer materials and labour on-site and a lot less project management. This results in houses being able to be built within just 4 weeks from the foundation stage. This is a game-changer because we want to be developers to work less and earn more, not to create ourselves a job, right!

There are also huge health and safety benefits on the site because more work is done offsite in a much safer environment. The construction industry is notorious for accidents, and 1 in 2 people will have a bad injury at some point in their career, and that's if their body lasts that long. I've been injured multiple times and even fallen through scaffolds three times in just one year, and remember I've never worked a full year since I was 19. With the trades' income relying on their bodies, it's important to look after everyone on your sites, and I'm a big believer that everyone should return home safely to their families after a day's work.

Some people still attach a stigma to prefab houses from those built after the war to be temporary; however, many of those have stood the test of time. Offsite construction has really advanced a long way over the past 10-20 years. There are now factories that have moved on from building panellised systems to now building fully volumetric systems. These are certain-size modules made of steel frame or timber frame which can be transported to the site on the back of a lorry. They are then craned off and installed by a few trades within less than an hour. These modules come fully finished inside, including the carpets, with all the external finishes completed.

Building with this type of system allows a developer to build two houses on-site and finish them within just 5-6 hours. Yes, you can build two houses without managing a single tradesman or material delivery once you have your groundworks in place. Because of the way the modules are craned in, you can have all your turf laid and driveway finished, meaning that people could move in at the end of the day. Imagine building this way next door to neighbours. You have just completed the foundations, your neighbours head off to work at 8 am, and by the time they get home from work at 5 pm, the houses are built and they have new neighbours moved in. It is bonkers to think about, but it is possible, and it is happening up and down the country on a daily basis. If building fully volumetric is so great, then why are we not building houses everywhere using this construction method?

The modular factories concentrate on doing pre-designed houses, meaning you get to choose from their product range rather than getting your architect to design a house every time you start a new site. Now this really makes sense because we only really build out a certain number of different house types and numbers of bedrooms, it's not as many as you may think. Every time your architect designs a house, it has to have structural calculations, be designed to be thermally efficient, be made so everything fits together, etc. It's only when you get on-site building the house that you know if it's going to actually work.

I've built over 200 houses, and there are problems with the design work many times, so if you use plans from something that's been built many times before, then this mitigates it every time you build. This is why the big house builders only have around 10 house types that they use on all their sites; they just change the materials, maybe build a detached garage instead of an attached one, change the porch, use render instead of brickwork, and so on. Ultimately, they stick to what they know, and this allows them to know exactly what a house will cost to build, right down to a penny because they've done so many of them.

We do a similar thing by using the same materials every time: bricks, roof tiles, window colour, paving slabs, fencing, kitchens, doors, tiles, aqua panels, mixer showers, taps, and even the plants. This saves us having to make decisions every time we build. Plus, we know where to buy the materials from and exactly what they cost. You have to take the personalisation out of it and get your developer's hat on. Keep things simple and give the market what they want.

As I mentioned at the beginning, no build system is perfect. The factories are expensive to set up and run. Therefore, they have a lot more overhead compared to building in a field. The factories are limited by how many houses they can build in a year. So, they can't fulfil the real demand for house builders. The modular factories are there. They can build the houses which are made to a really high standard with zero snagging. And yes, they are mortgageable, which is the most important thing. They just need to be able to ramp up production. The faster they can build, the cheaper the houses will cost to build.

The main point of this step is for you to understand that there are lots of different build systems available to you right now, and it's about finding the right system for your site. Things are changing all the time, so keep an open mind and always look at anything new. There are many companies that got left behind because they were stuck in their ways and weren't open to change. Companies such as:

HMV Music - They were offered iTunes, turned it down, and insisted people wanted to visit their stores and listen to the music before purchasing. iTunes had this covered by letting them listen to 1 minute for free online. So they went on to dominate the download music industry.

Blockbuster videos - Insisted that people wanted to rent their physical videos and DVDs, charged handsomely for late returns, which was their real business model. Netflix created a subscription model where you could watch films instantly with no late fees or having to drive to a physical shop. So they dominated the industry.

Kodak - One of the biggest companies in the world at one point lost out to phones having cameras on them. Where you could see if the picture you just took actually came out. If not, take it again and at no cost. The social media world is driven by images taken from phones and shared instantly. Kodak should've released a camera with a phone on it, which is what we all really have these days, rather than a phone with a camera on it.

IBM computers - Failed to adjust to the personal computer market. Microsoft saw the need from the market to have a personal computer in every house and dominated with rapid growth.

The Tie Rack - Failed to understand men's shopping habits and only sold a limited amount of items in physical stores with expensive overheads. Online retailers thrived, along with dropshipping, Amazon, and eBay, who had the ability to serve customers worldwide for a lot less cost.

These are just a few of the big companies, but many smaller ones go bust regularly also. Don't let this be you; embrace the future of construction and stay one step ahead of the competition.

Summary

1. Panelised systems can save you a lot of time on-site and reduce setting out mistakes, which are usually found out later when it's more expensive to rectify them.

2. Building offsite reduces labour and material delivery on-site, meaning a lot fewer things for you to manage.

3. Building offsite allows you to build quicker, resulting in interest savings and greater profits for you, the developer.

4. Building quicker allows you to roll your profits over into another development, making even greater profits. These systems fit well with the saying "Time is money."

5. Different build systems suit different conditions, such as working in wet weather. Choosing the right system could mean working regardless of the conditions compared to sites that come to a standstill when it rains or it's too cold.

6. Using offsite construction is good for fixed-price packages that can ensure you against huge price fluctuations that we've been seeing over the past few years.

7. Having a large chunk of the work done for you means you can

concentrate on looking for more sites and raising money, two of your key result areas.

8. Trades can work inside and outside on timber frame houses, rather than waiting for one trade to finish at a time like traditional construction.

9. With modular construction, you only have to manage two contracts: the groundworkers and the modular factory.

10. Modular construction allows you to build a house in just one day using predesigns. New factories are being built each year, so find a factory to suit your developments.

CHAPTER TEN

Getting your site Built

"If you think you can or you can't, you're absolutely right" - **Henry Ford.**

The final step of the Property Developers Blueprint is to build out the development. This is actually the easiest and most enjoyable part for most people, especially if you are a tradesman like me and my sons. This is where there are lots of moving parts that run-in sequence, so it's important to get things done right.

Getting your site built out first requires getting good builders in. If you are going down the route of using a main contractor who undertakes all of the work, then you won't have to deal with individual trades or the managing of those people on a daily basis like we do. A main contractor will run, manage, and take responsibility for the site from the start, right up until the completion, known as the handover. You will pay more for the convenience of using a main contractor, but it can free up your time to concentrate on finding the next deal, which will make you more profit.

I converted an old office into 34 apartments on a site nearly 3 hours away. There was no way it was feasible for me to drive to the site and manage it on a daily basis, and then drive home again. I certainly didn't want to stay away in a hotel all week, not seeing my family, so it made sense to work with a main contractor who would manage the whole process over 9 months.

Although there was the usual work upfront to get to the point of starting the work, it only involved me going to the site once a month for a meeting and some lunch. This is why I love developments so much because you can have a well-paid lifestyle from this business rather than a busy job like 99% of the businesses out there. One of the biggest changes that got me off the tools from working 80-100 hour work weeks was leveraging other people to do the work, and a main contractor ticks that box a treat.

However, if you are looking to run your own developments, then you will need to make sure all the trades are suitable. If you're a tradesman like me, then you can do your trade yourself if you choose, and you will also most likely have many other trades in your phonebook. Even though I'm a bricklayer, I will usually get bricklaying gangs to come in on a price. I can be doing much better things with my time.

If you're not a tradesman or don't have any trades, it is still more than possible for you to run and manage your own sites, providing you find the right people. Asking for referrals can be a good place to start. I was always told it takes years to build a good reputation and minutes to lose it, which is probably seconds now with the speed of social media. You can ask friends, family, and through your social media platforms, which should hopefully see some recommendations come through.

One of the main things to consider when looking to use contractors is ensuring they have the right experience, but just as importantly, the right attitude, as you'll be working with some of these people over several months. Many a client and contractor fall out over extras, quality of work, payments, etc. This can be avoided by having a contract and clear terms set out before any work commences. Note I said "before," and not trying to sort this stuff out halfway through. It will be too late by then. Get contracts in place before any work commences and never go against this rule.

Always aim to get individual trades in rather than a general builder. We have all heard of the phrase "Jack of all trades, master of none." I'm not saying that a lot of people can't do several trades, but ideally, a plumber should be doing plumbing and an electrician should be doing electrics.

To avoid any clashes with payments, you can set out payments at certain stages and always go for a fixed price. There are general rates for all trades doing their work, so a carpenter may get £x for fitting a door lining, £x per linear meter for skirting and architraves. Bricklayers get paid per brick and block, and other trades will have their rates for their line of work.

Trades like to work this way rather than being on day work clock-watching or doing £300 worth of work and getting paid £200 a day. There is never a shortage of tradespeople who prefer to be on day work and drag out their breaks and the work. Use these people at your own peril because they will cost you more money in the long run. This works the other way, whereby you could be paying someone £200 a day and they only do £100 of work. This means things can soon cost you double.

Most contractors should be busy and booked up several months in advance. If they are available to work straight away, then this could be a warning sign. Sometimes jobs do get delayed or cancelled, so I appreciate that some trades do become available all of a sudden. But make sure you check out if this is the case and take a look at their reviews.

I see so many people in the building game who never use a contract, which is madness. Contracts are there to protect you and the client, which is possibly going to be you. It's all very well doing things on a handshake or via an email, but these are big numbers not to do things correctly. The lenders will want to see a contract in place before they lend anyway.

I mentioned earlier that it takes 26 weeks to build a house. This is just an average guide, as houses come in all shapes and sizes, and factors such as roads can affect the timeframe for each site. It is essential to have a timeline to follow, so you know the sequence of trades, how long they will be on site, and what materials they will need in advance. You cannot keep this information in your head with all the other things you have going on. If a trade does not show up, it can have a significant impact on everyone else's schedule. Tradespeople are busy, so giving them plenty of notice is essential, especially if you need to reschedule them a few days later.

The program can also help you determine when to order materials for the site. This is crucial to avoid any delays. Some trades work on a day-to-day basis and do not mind waiting around for materials if they are getting paid. However, trades working on a fixed price might get frustrated and leave to work for someone who is more organised if they cannot get started. It can be challenging to get them back, causing significant delays.

All construction projects fall under Construction Design Management (CDM). Even if you are only replacing a sink in someone's property, CDM regulations apply. These regulations have been implemented to protect the welfare of workers and other individuals on the construction site, including customers. The principal designer, principal contractor, contractors, and workers all have CDM responsibilities that they must adhere to by law.

These responsibilities include aspects such as working at heights, controlling dust and noise, and proper manual handling techniques, to name a few. I often see people on social media undertaking extension, refurbishment, conversion, and new build projects, and I can confidently say that over 90% of them are not complying with their CDM responsibilities, or they may not even know what CDM is, which is quite shocking. As someone who has climbed some of the highest mountains in the world, I know a thing or two about taking risks, but the rules still apply to me, you, and all workers. I am particular about ensuring that extension leads do not pose trip hazards, that dust is properly suppressed, and that no one lifts something too heavy on their own. Dust can be a significant cause of illness, and even asbestos can be a killer in the construction industry.

Many people undertake jobs involving the removal of pipes, coving, artex, storage heaters, etc., but they often do not check if these items contain asbestos. Asbestos was a cheap building material commonly used from the 1930s to the 1980s, with the 1960s and onwards being the most popular period. Interestingly, the biggest victims of asbestos exposure years ago were not the workers using asbestos but rather their wives. The wives used to shake off the dust from the workers' clothes before putting them in the washing machine, unknowingly inhaling asbestos fibres day after day and suffering the consequences as a result.

Throughout the build, there will be inspections by quite a few people, such as Building Control, your warranty provider, QS, Project Monitoring Surveyor, Health and Safety consultant, and Project Manager. Make sure they visit at the relevant stages throughout the build, or they won't do the final sign-offs, which could cause all sorts of complications and delays at the sale stage. The visits can involve seeing how much work has been completed before releasing payments to checking that the work is compliant throughout the build.

Some inspectors are more thorough than others, and it may take a project or two to build the trust of the inspector to see that you are doing things properly. Just having your site tidy at all times makes a big impression. The last thing you want is unnecessary delays in the sale, resulting in paying more for your finance and not getting paid your profits later than expected if the inspections are not ready or if work fails and needs remediating.

One of the great things about being a developer is the legacy you leave behind. This doesn't just involve building amazing, high-quality homes for people to live in, but you can also get to name your streets after your loved ones. We've named one after my late father-in-law, Leonard's Close, to whom I dedicate this book, and another recent one after my mother-in-law, Carmela Close. This makes my sons really proud of the houses they build. Now, there is no promise you can name a street after your loved ones if there is already an existing street with the same name, but it's a lovely touch and something I highly recommend you do if you get the chance.

While we trust the trades to do the job that we've paid them for and also to have good intentions to keep an eye on everyone throughout the build, there will inevitably be some niggly bits known as snags. As discussed earlier, most trades will be working on a price and work at a good speed, which can sometimes cause a drop in quality. Or other trades cause minor damage to finished work. This obviously can't be left as is, and you don't want the homeowners to be getting you back to rectify things when they are living in the property. So, the best thing to do is to make the time to check on the work, ask your trades to rectify things while they are on site, have their tools and materials, as this will be a lot easier to do now rather than later. The homeowners will walk around with a snagging list before they complete the purchase, so you may as well eliminate all of them as soon as possible.

Some of the big housebuilders can build 2-3 houses a week on large sites, and when the market is heated and sales are coming thick and fast, the developer can be under immense pressure to get them completed by a certain date. It's easier to pay someone to rectify these snags afterward rather than build slowly. It's not the way we like to do things; we prefer to build them right in the first place and hand them over snag-free. Then, you avoid callbacks and disgruntled customers.

Every new property must have a 10-year structural warranty. This is an insurance policy that, should something go significantly wrong later down the line, provides protection for the homeowner and the developer. The warranty covers the structural element of the building, not things like a door handle breaking. This is for you, the developer (or your main contractor), to address in the first 2 years of the warranty. As with anything that costs money, you need to shop around. If you're comparing prices, just make sure that everything is included on all quotes, as some may seem cheap and miss things off the policy.

Congratulations! You've just built your first of many developments, and it's now time to sell the property if this is your chosen exit strategy. In most cases, we will sell the properties through the agent we purchased the land with. This is great for the agent as they get more than just the one fee they got when they sold you the land. If you're building 5 houses, then the agent would receive 6 fees. This will incentivise them to bring you more land before it comes on to the market.

I often get asked if they should sell through a single agent or multi agency, and to be honest, there is no right or wrong answer. If you build the right house in the right location that the market wants, like the Property Developers Blueprint advises, then a sole agent should be sufficient; their fees will be lower than multi-agents also.

We usually finish our builds completely before we allow viewings. We have sold off-plan before, which can be great to have some degree of certainty. This involves marketing the properties at the foundation stage, or even earlier. The problems arise with timing the build for your buyers as most sales take 8-10 weeks, whereas your build will take more than 26 weeks. Buyers can also keep coming to a site, which is a dangerous place as discussed earlier, and they will start to treat you like their builder doing a self-build. They ask for loads of extras, then change their minds, and this can be just like working for customers again. So, we find finishing the sites is better, and usually, the first 1 or 2 people who walk through the door will want to buy it because they can see everything finished and it is ready to move straight in.

When you finally sell the property, it can be a real mix of emotions because it has taken a lot of work, money, and time to get to this point. But this is where your 6 or 7-figure profit lands in your bank. Investors and lenders are all paid back with their interest as promised, and now your bank balance has just had 10, 20, or 30+ years of your usual hard-earned income land in it in just one go. That makes more of a difference to your life than any cash-flowing strategy that I know of. This money could mean lots of different things to you, but whatever it is, I would urge you to do this very valuable exercise right now and write down a list of all the things you would buy or do if the following amounts were to land in your bank today. I've also put some of the most common ones as examples that my mentees have used.

£100,000

- Pay off some of or all of your debts.
- Pay off the mortgage or a big chunk of it.
- Take the pressure off paying your bills.
- Stop working on the tools.
- Have some cash in the bank for the first time in your life.
- Treat the family to a nice holiday.

£250,000

- Buy a nice car.
- Work just 6+ months a year.
- Allow your partner to quit their job.
- Become your own bank.
- Treat the family to multiple holidays.
- Help your kids get started.

£500,000

- Buy a holiday home abroad.
- Pay off your parents' mortgage.
- Bring family members into your business.
- Use main contractors all the time.
- Spend a lot of time on your hobbies.

£1,000.000+

- Live abroad whilst doing developments in the UK.
- Become an investor for 50% of the profits without doing any of the work.
- Give a lot back to charity with time and money.
- Retirement.
- Dream cars.
- Dream holidays.
- Perfect lifestyle.

The reason I want you to do this exercise is because if you do not know what you would do with these amounts of money, then you'll never have enough reasons to go out and earn it in the first place. A great thing to do that has worked for me is to create a vision board and put it in a place you will see every day. Put images of all the things you want to do and buy without limiting yourself to what these things cost. Get your family involved also so you know you are all on the same page and you will all benefit from the results of this strategy and the work it takes.

One thing you may encounter when you earn life-changing money is that people you know will say you've changed, and they will most likely be right because money gives you options and makes you more of who you already are. If you're a generous, caring person you will just help and care more. If you're a hard worker, you'll still work hard, but on the things you want to do and enjoy doing. Simply put, money will allow you to be yourself, something that many people have forgotten to do with the cost of living and just how busy we make ourselves these days.

Summary

1. Decide if you want to build out the site yourself or use a main contractor for leverage.

2. Get recommendations for tradespeople that you want to use who have good reputations.

3. Choose a build system that suits the site, think about using a system that saves you time.

4. You must ensure that you and the workers all comply with CDM regulations.

5. Ensure you have all the right inspectors in at the relevant stages.

6. Make sure all the work is complete when the inspectors come out as this could cause delays and cost money.

7. Don't skip getting contracts in place before you get the tradespeople on site.

8. Use the program to get labour and materials on site in the right sequence.

9. Find a good agent who is very proactive in selling your properties so you can get your life-changing profit as soon as possible.

10. Know exactly what you will do with the money once your profits hit your bank. This will really fuel you to become a property developer.

CHAPTER ELEVEN

Case studies

"Our greatest weakness lies in giving up. The most certain way to succeed is always to try just one more time" **- Thomas Edison.**

For those of you who follow me on social media, you will see us start and finish a site each year, spend winters abroad, and enjoy our profits. A big part of what I do is teach and mentor others from all walks of life to do the same. So let's look at some case studies from people who were sitting there thinking about property development as a strategy not too long ago, have gone out, implemented what they have learned by following the Property Developers Blueprint, and reaped the rewards.

Henry Bramell and Lee Bramell

Henry and Lee have done an amazing job on their first build. Henry was a busy electrician working for customers before he did the Property Developers Blueprint. He then quit and went into developments full-time, paying himself a project manager's fee each month. He also carried out a variety of other building work for his customers, which he has put these skills to good use on his own build.

Henry managed to locate a back garden plot with planning just a few houses away from where his dad lives. They sold their flat and moved into his dad's so they could save money and be right next to the build. This is a prime example of being prepared to go backwards to move forwards.

Henry worked on the project daily with a good friend. He has done 80% of the work and realised he needs to leverage more on their next site to speed things up. One thing that was impressive is Henry building the timber frame himself. This took 1 month and saved him £20,000. Not bad for a month's work on your own project.

They already have a second site for 1 bungalow in a large garden plot, brought to them via their architect, which they are hoping to start on in the spring. Henry and Lee have recently returned from spending 6 weeks in Spain over Christmas and plan to return next winter for longer after they've completed their next site.

They funded both projects through family, friends, their own money, and my broker bringing in the money for the build.

Company - Bramell Homes Ltd

Development - 1 x 4 bed detached

Location - Burwash, East Sussex

Purchase price - £200,000

GDV - £800,000

Build cost including fees - £375,000

Profit - £175,000

Build time - 15 months

Challenges - Rising building materials and labour costs. Interest rate rises. Expensive utilities.

Henry and Lee's three top tips:

1. Don't try to do it all yourself, employ subcontractors who do their trade every day.

2. Be prepared to make sacrifices for the first project or two. Roll your sleeves up and do a few late nights and weekends – it is well worth it from the rewards you'll get.

3. Get educated and mentored, as this will save you from making mistakes. Watch YouTube, network, do courses and learn as much as you can.

Contact information

info@bramallhomes.co.uk

www.bramallhomes.co.uk

Sean Parker and Paul Grears

Sean and Paul are bricklayers by trade who were building extensions for customers before they did the Property Developers Blueprint. They are always very busy and decided they might as well be busy working on their own projects.

Sean and Paul are now about to start their second project of another large house refurbishment and extension. They've also gained planning for a detached bungalow in the rear garden belonging to the house.

They also have another project of three bungalows that they are taking through the planning process. They've managed to raise the money for all three projects from three of their previous customers who have gotten to know them from working around their houses so they like their work and approach to quality and doing things right.

Sean has recently attended my business planning retreat in Cyprus, where we spent a week with a small group of like-minded people working on his one, three, and five-year business plans to take his business to the next level.

Company - Parker Grears Developments Ltd

Development - 1 house with extension and full refurbishment

Location - Nuneaton

Purchase price - £277,500

GDV - £423,000

Build cost including fees - £90,000

Profit - £60,000

Build time - 6 months

Challenges - Getting a build over agreement from Severn Trent. Time to arrange their finances and legal documents. Changing things in the plans and doing retrospective planning.

Sean and Paul's three top tips:

1. Make sure you have a good solicitor that understands commercial purchases, and is quick to respond to any queries.

2. Plan ahead for everything in great detail to avoid delays.

3. Don't give up and be persistent. It is a rollercoaster of ups and downs, but if you practice what Andy teaches then it definitely pays off.

Contact information

parkergrears@gmail.com

www.parkergrears.com

Frank Garvey and Laraine Pearn

Frank and Laraine have completed several projects after Frank decided to cease working for other builders and customers for £200 a day. They both obtained plots by purchasing 2 houses that they now rent out.

They have undertaken most of the work themselves, in addition to hiring other trade subcontractors. Frank still has a strong passion for bricklaying and is currently supporting his grandson Harley in his bricklaying apprenticeship, which is a wonderful sight to see. Frank often visits our sites and lays bricks to spend time with me and my sons.

Frank and Laraine's vision is to construct their dream villa in Lanzarote and indulge in their love for mountain biking. They have recently acquired a building plot in Lanzarote with stunning sea views. Over time, we have developed a close friendship and have spent the past 2 Christmas holidays mountain biking together in Lanzarote.

Frank and Laraine have attended 4 retreats, 3 in Tenerife and 1 in Cyprus. They have already booked their 5th retreat, which will be in Tenerife in 2025. Prior to attending the retreats in January, they spend 5 weeks mountain biking in Lanzarote before taking a short flight over to Tenerife.

Company - Iprospect Homes Ltd

Development 1 - 1 x 3 bed bungalow

Development 2 - 1 x 3 bed house

Location - Rochdale, Lancashire

Purchase price Development 1 - £0 (Land for free)

GDV - £251,000

Build cost including fees - £105,000

Profit - £146,000

Build time - £12 months

Purchase price development 2 - £0 (Land for free)

GDV - £265,000

Build cost including fees - £131,000

Profit - £134,000

Build time - 12 months

Project pipeline

1. Planning in principle for 8-9 bungalows in Rochdale.
2. Commercial to residential conversion into 8 flats and another 4 in airspace in Rochdale.

3. Full planning for 6 bungalows in Lancashire.

Challenges - Getting planning permission refused, then won 11 months later during an appeal. Raising private equity, but we did it. This came from one of Andy's mentees in his private Facebook group.

Frank and Laraine's three top tips:

1. Find a plot in a good location, with good access.
2. Be realistic with your budget.
3. Get your planning permission and warranties in order, then find a good architect and planning consultant.

Contact information

Facebook - Frank Garvey

Instagram - Iprospecthomes

Adam Hall and Dave Richardson

Adam and Dave run a successful high-end aluminium glazing business called Sightline. Since doing the Property Developers Blueprint, they've managed to step out of their business and have a team running the whole thing, allowing them to fully focus on developments full-time.

They have worked closely with one of my architects and solicitors to secure several sites and have recently completed their first build.

Adam and Dave like working directly with vendors, working closely with their power team and taking the sites through to full planning. On their first build, they were fairly hands-on labouring and supporting their subcontractors so they could learn more about how all the trades work and create a good build team that they can work with on a regular basis.

Company - Richardson and Hall Luxury Developments

Development - 1 x 3 bedroom detached house

Location - Earl Shilton, Leicestershire

Purchase price - £55,000

GDV - £295,000

Build cost including fees - £150,000

Profit - £90,000

Build time - 5+ months

Challenges - Long drainage run of 50 metres to connect into the main drains, reducing the ground level by about 1m to start the foundations.

Pipeline of deals

Next project due to start is 3 detached bungalows

8 houses in legals

Adam and Dave's three top tips:

1. Check all utilities and costs to bring them to the site.
2. Make sure you have a solid team around you on and off site.
3. Make sure you have a pipeline of deals, as things may take longer and you may get delays.

Contact information

Facebook - Richardson and Hall Developments

Instagram - Richardson and Hall Developments

Matthew Brewer

Company - Elderbrook Homes

Development - 1 x 3 bedroom detached house

Location - Suffolk

Purchase price - £155,000

GDV - £650,000

Build cost including fees - £320,000

Profit - £115,000

Build time - 7 months

Challenges - Securing the plot at the right price. My own mental block was asking people to invest their money in me and my projects, but I eventually got out of my own way and got the money.

Pipeline of deals

1 site in for planning for 2 detached houses in Suffolk

Land with 2 plots accepted in Suffolk

Option agreement secured for barn conversion in Suffolk

Further deals in negotiations

Matt's three top tips:

1. Find the right site and agree on the right price. It's a numbers game. Meet the agents, get the offers in and build relationships. Be persistent as some deals can take a while to get over the line.

2. You don't need to be wealthy and have all the money to buy the land. Get some training and understand how the process and finance works.

3. Team up with someone that has the same values and opposite skill sets. Especially if you're working full time - you can share the workload.

Contact information

matt@elderbrookhomes.co.uk

www.elderbrookhomes.co.uk

Tom Davenport

Company - T and I Homes

Development - Barn conversion into 3 units

Location - Somerset

Purchase price - £535,000

GDV - £2,300,000

Build cost including fees - £625,523

Fees and finance - £207,883

Profit - £931,594

Build time - 9 months

Challenges - Reliable investors but got several in the end. Lenders asking questions ate into the deal.

Pipeline of deals

1 Barn conversion + several other barns on 5 acres. GDV £8,276,000 with a profit of £3,149,184

Full planning for 5 and looking to gain another 5, on the other part of the land units. GDV £4,700,000 with a profit of £1,113,132.

Tom's three top tips:

1. Stay resilient even when it gets tough. You get through everything eventually.

2. Seek help from a skilled team. This helps identify things I may have missed. A skilled team can help you bring the project in on time and on budget.

3. Know your strengths and weaknesses. It took me a while to figure this out. A mentor like Andy Hubbard is priceless for this and has taught me an enormous amount.

Contact information

info@tihomes.co.uk

Facebook - T&I Homes Ltd/Thomas Davenport

Mike Prentice

Company - Beacon Eco Homes

Development - 1 x 5 bedroom executive detached house

Location - Llandybie, South Wales

Purchase price - £115,000

GDV - £575,000

Build cost including fees - £250,000

Profit - £175,000

Build time - 9 months

Challenges - Finance took longer than anticipated but got there eventually. Building to exceed current building regulations to achieve a passive house rating. This has added additional costs and time, but this was a choice from us, not planning or building regs.

Pipeline of deals

We bought a 15-acre site taking it through to full planning for 90 units, which we will sell on for a multi-7-figure profit.

An option agreement on land for 50 units, that we will take through planning.

Just going through legals to build a 3-bedroom-bungalow in March 2024.

In talks with another developer for joint venture on a scheme of 8 x 4 bedroom detached houses, to start early 2025.

Mike's top three tips:

1. Things take longer than anticipated, especially on your first development.

2. Make sure you are organised, as there are a lot of moving parts and people to deal with.

3. Stay in work to keep the cash flow coming in, until your first deal is complete. You can then go full time whilst the next deal pays out. There is a lot of work involved, but it's a short-erm sacrifice for life-changing money, so never give up.

Contact information

mike@selouhomes.co.uk

www.beaconecohomes.co.uk

As you can see from these case studies, they have all persisted in making their dreams come true by pursuing their own projects. I thought it would be useful and transparent to show you some of their challenges and tips to help you understand that the rewards are well worth the required work, and that there is indeed work required. You're probably already working hard anyway, so you may as well work hard on your own development and get paid 10, 20, or even 30+ times more than what you are earning right now.

If you enjoyed reading these case studies, and you would like to see many more, simply head over to www.developinghomes.co.uk/case-studies/.

CHAPTER TWELVE

What next?

"If someone offers you an amazing opportunity and you're not sure you can do it, just say 'yes' then learn how to do it later" - **Sir Richard Branson.**

Now that we've been through the 8 steps of the Property Developers Blueprint system, it's time to get out there and take some action. This may feel daunting, and you won't know where to begin or what to do first. Maybe you need more help and education? Maybe you want to learn more?

There's only so much information we can fit into this book, which is why we have the Property Developers Blueprint online course, the only online property development course available in the UK. This course has over 130 in-depth videos and documents that will give you the confidence to get out there and talk like a seasoned developer, something that many fear when they enter the estate agents for the first time.

The comprehensive online course also includes the exact deal analyser that I've mentioned throughout this book and the one I use, which allows you to appraise a site in minutes rather than hours. This deal analyser has allowed me to secure deals that other people couldn't, even if they offered a higher price, and of course, it has earned me hundreds of thousands of pounds.

Included in the online course is a checklist when looking at land. This checklist ensures you don't miss anything off when looking at land and avoid the mistakes other developers make. The checklist allows you to identify any concerns which can be used as negotiation tools as discussed earlier in the book.

We also have a private Facebook Support Group for anyone who buys the online Property Developers Blueprint course. This group is full of hundreds of like-minded people who you can connect with instantly. Some of those people will be investors looking to invest in people's deals, who knows, it might be yours next? There are power team members, trades, contractors, solicitors, everyone you will need to support you on your journey in that private group. You can also ask any questions you have in the group and get them answered, which is a game-changer. If you need to discuss a conversation with a vendor, check some build costs, see if your offer pack looks great, then you have the ability to do that within this special group.

"What if things change though?" you might ask yourself. We want to give you as much value as possible, which is why the online course comes with free lifetime updates. This means if we add in more content or renew existing content, you'll get this automatically, and it will never be out of date. I already have plans to add more things to the online course later this year that will improve your chances of success.

I'm all for action takers, and as an added bonus, I'd like to offer you an exclusive discount only to everyone who has bought and read this book. If you enter the coupon code **'Book100'** at the checkout, you'll get £100+ VAT off any online or live course as a way of my appreciation for your support.

Here's the link to see what's included in the online Property Developers

Blueprint. You can purchase the course on the same link also and gain immediate access to start learning the content:

online.developinghomes.co.uk/pdb

Or maybe you prefer attending live seminars, asking your questions in person, and networking face to face with like-minded people? You're in luck as I also run 3-day live Property Developers Blueprint events, usually in Peterborough. I love meeting people and seeing them arrive as one person and leave 3 days later with clarity, goals, a better mindset, and enthusiasm. If you would like to attend, then you can see what's included and book your seat via the link below:

live.developinghomes.co.uk/pdb-live

Whether you choose to do the online course, attend a live event, or go it alone, don't let finishing this book be the end of your quest to become a property developer and live life on your own terms. I haven't done anything that you or anyone else who's read this book cannot do themselves. There is nothing special about me, but there is something special about the system I have created. If you want something different, then you have to do something different. Invest the next 1-3 years into this strategy, and you will start living an amazing life.

You can make a difference in the world by building good-quality houses and keeping the economy going by supporting hundreds of people in their work. Building homes where people will be born, have birthdays, and enjoy parties with friends and loved ones is very powerful. You will always be so much more than just another developer.

Just make sure you don't walk away from opportunities like I did when I met my mentors 9 years earlier. Ignoring that opportunity to work with them cost me millions of pounds in lost opportunities, which meant I spent many weeks working 80-100 hours a week, hard in the wrong direction, when I didn't have to. All this while being away from my family. Valuable time that I will unfortunately never get back.

I'd love to hear your success stories like the ones we featured in the previous chapter, so please feel free to drop me an email at info@developinghomes. co.uk and let's celebrate the wins together. It would also be great to connect with you and follow your journeys, as well as you seeing our latest developments on my socials below:

Facebook - developinghomes

Instagram - developinghomes

TikTok - developing_homes

Website - www.developinghomes.co.uk

YouTube - Developing Homes

Andy's Facebook - andrew.hubbard

Andy's Instagram - andyhubb30

Andy's TikTok - andyhubb30

Andy's LinkedIn - Andy Hubbard SMSTS

Andy's YouTube - Andy Hubbard

One last thing, I hope you found this book useful in many ways, and I would really appreciate it if you could leave a review on Amazon. These reviews really help this book reach other people who want to become property developers and change their lives, and you would be doing your part to help create much-needed homes. Thank you.

ABOUT THE AUTHOR

Andy Hubbard

From humble beginnings, growing up in a rented house, failing at school, and working as a bricklayer, to becoming the UK's best property development trainer and mentor, a multimillionaire, and a multi-stage ultra runner, Andy's journey is a testament to the transformative power of hard work, mindset, and dedication.

After working too hard for far too long, dreaming of retirement and escaping the daily grind, Andy invested multiple six figures in his own education, personal development, and mentors. Now, he gets to live a life of freedom and choice on his own terms.

When Andy isn't on one of his development sites or training and mentoring his students, he can be found pursuing his passion for travelling the world with his family, climbing mountains, catching huge fish, or running across deserts to raise money for charity.

Andy lives by his motto, *"If someone else can do that, then so can I."* He never puts a limit on what he wants to achieve, which means he and his family get to live an extraordinary life, and you can too.

Printed in Great Britain
by Amazon

41619081R00096